PENGUIN BOOKS

PORTRAIT OF AN OLD LADY

Stephen Fay became editor of *Business* magazine in 1986, having spent most of his life as a reporter on the *Sunday Times*. Born in Rochdale in 1938, he was the son of a distinguished reporter on the *Manchester Guardian*. He went to school in London and university in New Brunswick, Canada. Stephen Fay first worked as a journalist for the *Glasgow Herald*, and joined the *Sunday Times* in 1964. In the next twenty years he covered the United States (as New York and then Washington Correspondent) and the EEC; he was labour correspondent and the last of the legitimate line of Atticus. He also wrote extensively about the theatre and opera.

His books include *Beyond Greed, or The Great Silver Bubble*, the story of an attempt to corner the world silver market. He is co-author of *Hoax!: The Inside Story of the Howard Hughes – Clifton Irving Affair*, which won an Edgar from the Mystery Writers of America as the best non-fiction mystery of 1972. His account of an ill-fated production of Wagner's *Ring* in Bayreuth appeared in 1984.

Stephen Fay is married with two children. They live in Islington, London.

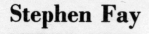

Stephen Fay

PORTRAIT
OF AN OLD LADY

Turmoil at the Bank of England

PENGUIN BOOKS

PENGUIN BOOKS

Published by the Penguin Group
27 Wrights Lane, London W8 5TZ, England
Viking Penguin Inc., 40 West 23rd Street, New York, New York 10010, USA
Penguin Books Australia Ltd, Ringwood, Victoria, Australia
Penguin Books Canada Ltd, 2801 John Street, Markham, Ontario, Canada L3R 1B4
Penguin Books (NZ) Ltd, 182–190 Wairau Road, Auckland 10, New Zealand

Penguin Books Ltd, Registered Offices: Harmondsworth, Middlesex, England

First published by Viking 1987
Published in Penguin Books, with a new final chapter, 1988

Made and printed in Great Britain by
Richard Clay Ltd, Bungay, Suffolk
Filmset in Bodoni

For Professor W. Y. Smith, of the University of
New Brunswick, from whom I first learned about the connection
between moral suasion and central banking

Contents

Author's Note

This portrait of the Bank of England is not official or authorized. However, it could not have been written without the Bank's cooperation. Officials at all levels were encouraged to speak freely to me, and, in return, I agreed to check with them any direct quotations. These could be altered only to correct grammar or to achieve greater clarity. Without ever being sure what conclusions I might draw, the Bank's officials displayed admirable candour and considerable generosity throughout this inquiry.

In his introduction to Chapter 1 of *Lombard Street*, Walter Bagehot wrote: 'A notion prevails that the money market is something so impalpable that it can only be spoken of in very abstract words, and that therefore books on it must be exceedingly difficult. But I maintain that money is as concrete and real as anything else: that it can be described in plain words; that it is the writer's fault if what he says is not clear.'

I have tried to achieve such a standard of clarity, and if I have not done so, it is not the fault of anyone but myself.

Stephen Fay
London, March 1988

Prologue: A Crisis of Identity

In the summer of 1980, Gordon Richardson was in his prime. Among the qualities demanded of the Governor of the Bank of England, authority is the one that matters most, and Richardson exuded authority. He had already been in office for seven years, and had become confident of his command of the business of central banking. That summer, he spoke about central bankers in a way both gnomic and deft, by comparing the games of cricket and squash. The occasion of this comment was the opening of new squash courts at the Bank of England's ample playing-fields in the London suburb of Roehampton, and the speech is fully recorded only in the official history of the Bank's sports club. It deserves a wider audience.

The trouble with cricket, Richardson explained, is that it is uneconomical of manpower, that it takes up too much land and that it is riddled with restrictive practices; for example, in the batting side, only two people are actually playing the game while the others stand or even sit idly around. This is a central banker's nightmare. Squash, on the other hand, employs only two people who play very hard for a short period of time and then pass the court on to other players. 'Squash,' he continued, 'like the City of London, depends largely on self-regulation. Just as in this country we have no bank inspectors and no Securities and Exchange Commission, so squash players generally sort out their differences without the need for the referee's whistle or the umpire's white coat.' The game demands efficiency, hard work, discipline and gentlemanly behaviour – a central banker's dream.

Richardson's speech contained an inference that he did not need to spell out to that audience. It was this: should the need for rules and umpiring decisions in the City arise, the central bankers of the Bank of England were admirably equipped to lend a hand. After all it was run by a Governor who was thoughtful, decisive and secure enough in the job to be able to describe central banking as a game.

For that reason it is not as frivolous as it might seem to begin an inquiry into the Bank of England at the sports club, especially as the ground reflects the way in which the Bank likes to think of itself, being discreet and set behind a ring of fine tall trees. Standards of dress and decorum are high, and there are no concessions to meretricious modernism: no slot machines in the bar. There is no need to boast about it. Well kept and efficiently run, it is simply the best of its kind.

There is no better day on which to see the ground than the Governor's cricket match, which, uneconomical though it may be, is held in July each year. The hedges that divide the twelve grass tennis-courts from the larger of two cricket fields are neatly clipped and the air is scented with cut grass. Wimbledon's qualifying matches are played on the best of those courts, and the England team practises on the football pitch beyond the courts. On the Sunday of the cricket match there are two taut white marquees in front of the pavilion, into which guests are invited for a glass of Pimms Cup. The match in progress is between the Bank's first team and an eleven chosen by the Governor; Richardson strengthened his team by the inclusion of a great professional cricketer, Tom Graveney. He was a non-playing captain, and I happened to see him then watching the play, standing slightly in front of the junior men, looking like a great landowner surveying his acreage. On the lawn in front of the pavilion young bank employees lay on the grass, finishing the lunch-time wine. Their wives and children were swimming in the large indoor pool, named after Lord O'Brien, Richardson's predecessor. It looked like an advertisement for life in England but published in America: a snapshot from the past; a picture of effortless confidence. Part of a mystery.

Some years later, when the chairman of the Bank of England sports club again requested the pleasure of my company on the occasion of the Governor's cricket match, the scene looked little different. The junior employees did seem a bit more boisterous after lunch, but the most significant change seemed to be that the Governor was actually playing. Dressed in a colourful blazer and cap, Robin Leigh-Pemberton looked entirely at home, chattering and laughing with other members of the team as they sat in canvas chairs by the boundary. He concentrated suitably hard as he played a few practice strokes at balls bowled by Colin Cowdrey, one of the great England batsmen, and a fellow man of Kent. (As it happened, Leigh-Pemberton scored nine not out that day, more than Colin Cowdrey.) But the maintenance of those old-fashioned standards had begun to look less effortless, more suspiciously contrived.

During the years since I had last visited the Governor's cricket match, Gordon Richardson's good run had come to an end. Having overcome the banking crisis of 1973–4, the sterling crisis of 1976 and the worst stretch of inflation in British history, he spent his last four years as Governor being lectured by the Prime Minister, Mrs Margaret Thatcher, while Treasury officials avenged themselves for slights they believed they had suffered during the years of the Governor's pre-

13

eminence. By the time he left the Bank in 1983 Richardson's reputation was immeasurably higher abroad than it was in Whitehall. Considering all he had done, that must have seemed unfair.

Robin Leigh-Pemberton was plucked, much to his surprise, from the chairmanship of the National Westminster Bank, and the only thing he had in common with Richardson was that they had both qualified as lawyers. He was not intended by Downing Street to exercise the same commanding influence as his predecessor. Leigh-Pemberton is blessed with a cheerful disposition, which is just as well, for after he had been little more than a year in office, on 30 September 1984, the Bank of England announced that it had organized the rescue of Johnson Matthey Bankers Limited. That was the beginning of an ordeal the Bank was ill-equipped to withstand, and (if central banking it to be thought of as a game) during that crisis the Bank of England watched victory being transformed into something like humiliating defeat.

Now, almost a decade after Richardson opened those squash courts, the City no longer regulates itself in a gentlemanly manner under the watchful gaze of the Governor. Not when the principal subjects of gossip are share-price manipulation, insider trading and preposterously high salaries. The players themselves are growing accustomed to settling differences in courts of law as they do in New York City, where many of them come from, and the Securities and Investments Board, established in 1986, bears a closer resemblance to the SEC in Washington DC than Richardson ever contemplated. In 1987 a tough new Banking Bill – amending the original 1979 Banking Act – enshrined the hurtful proposition that the Bank is helpless to stop a conspiracy of bankers. Its authority was no longer unquestioned and for the first time in its history its regulatory power had to be defined by written rules and enforced by the threat of judicial punishment.

The Bank of England is a most English institution, and is still capable of polished performances in the market-place as well as on the cricket field. Privately, however, it is an institution beset by anxiety: it is clearly not what it was, and is not certain what it will become. This book is not so much a portrait as a moving picture, intended to describe the origin and evolution of this crisis of identity.

1

Mystery on Threadneedle Street

It would be unprofitable to try and assess the condition of the Bank of England without knowing what happens behind the two great bronze doors at the main entrance in Threadneedle Street and the discreet sign reading 'No admittance, except on business'.

Standing on the other side of the heavy swing doors in the spacious entrance hall are gatekeepers dressed in the Bank's own livery: red waistcoats, pink tail coats and top hats. The head gatekeeper is a fine-looking man with a silver moustache named Arthur Pointer, whose father worked at the Bank and whose son is employed in another Bank building by St Paul's Cathedral. Pointer's job is to distinguish between people who are merely curious ('We'll let them photograph us on the front step if we're not too busy'), people who have business in the Bank and people who think they have. There are, for instance, regular visits from people whose banknotes have been mutilated, since the Bank makes them and must replace damaged notes: 'The wife's put her husband's trousers in the washing machine when he hasn't told her he's had a win at the dogs,' explains Pointer by way of an example. Or a tramp, exhibiting some sense of humour, comes in and asks for money. The head gatekeeper is diplomatic and treats them all tolerantly. 'You're a bit like an ambassador,' he says. So he is always polite when persons walk in off the street and ask to open an account, referring them to a commercial bank, like Lloyds across Royal Exchange Place. This is because the Bank of England is hardly a 'bank' at all, in any common meaning of the word.

There are few exceptions to the rule about accounts. Chancellors of the Exchequer can have chequing accounts (Roy Jenkins and Lord Barber did; James Callaghan did not). The Corporation of the City of London banks at the Bank, and the privilege is also extended to Lord Mayors of London. A few profoundly well-established companies have accounts, and discover that the rarity of a cheque drawn on the Bank of England has a fringe benefit: some sentimental recipients prefer to keep them uncashed. Most of the comparatively few personal accounts, however, are opened by the Bank's staff. Until recently, the Bank denied them overdrafts, declaring them to be imprudent: any employee whose account was overdrawn received a visit from the manager ten minutes after the close of business. This unbending attitude lasted until the Bank discovered that many members of the staff were transferring their accounts to better-disposed bankers. But the old discipline was more revealing of the Bank, which is not actually in the business of banking – it is not there to make money by lending to individual customers.

Employees of the Bank of England are not to be confused with the general run of City bankers. They are central bankers; the rest are commercial bankers. Central bankers regard themselves as public servants (although they expect to be paid more than mere civil servants) for the Bank is the government's banker. Of course, the business is different from any normal banker-client relationship. After all, the customer owns the bank. But there are vestiges of the disciplined attitudes bankers once wished to impart to their clients. Successive Governors of the Bank of England described their role as 'custodians of the nation's currency'. In that capacity, the Bank can behave as though it has a moral responsibility to prevent the government from behaving improvidently. A more prosaic interpretation of the Bank's role is contained in one of its *Bulletins*: 'As the central bank of the United Kingdom the Bank are primarily and fundamentally concerned with the nation's money.' This was written before the Bank ceased to be plural. It was the Governor and Company of the Bank of England – plural – until the late 1970s, when the decision was taken to regard the Bank, once and for all, as a singular institution.

The Bank in the plural was a grammatical contribution to the legend of the Bank. It was by no means the first bank, but by the nineteenth century it confidently asserted that it was the most influential, and this was not just idle conceit. This was part of the mystique of the Bank of England, designed to encourage the concept of its authority. Its authority gave the Bank its power, and it is useful, therefore, to establish the basic outline of its history.

Although none of the official histories says so, the motives that inspired the foundation of the Bank in 1694 were fear and greed. In the City the reign of Charles II was distinguished by his decision to appropriate the assets of London's goldsmiths. From then on the City equated the Stuart line with embezzlement. Of course, the merchants did not approve of the revolution that brought William III to the throne, and were reluctant to extend him any credit, but when it looked as though the new Protestant king might lose the French wars because he could not afford to fight them, the merchants began to weigh their options more carefully. If the French won, James II would be restored to the throne, putting the City's assets at risk again.

17

Moreover, the new king needed credit so badly that it ought to be possible to make a turn on the deal.

The Bank of England was founded to raise £1,200,000 for the king at a perpetual rate of interest of 8 per cent. The original subscribers are listed in a ledger in the Bank's museum, and there is a high proportion of Protestant Huguenot names amongst them. Sir John Houblon, the first Governor, was a Huguenot, and one of the Bank's agreeable myths is that the red waistcoats and pink coats are the livery of Sir John's own servants. In return the king gave the government's account to the new Bank, whose founders judged shrewdly that the size of the government account would attract considerable private business. The convenient concept of limited liability was also extended to the Company; a further inducement was the right to print banknotes.

It was an excellent deal. The Bank quickly installed itself in the City, overcoming its first great crisis in 1720, when its credit was almost wiped out by the South Sea Bubble. By 1797 it was so thoroughly established that the playwright Richard Brinsley Sheridan could refer to the Bank crossly as 'an elderly lady in the City', a phrase which was transformed by the cartoonist James Gilray into 'The Old Lady of Threadneedle Street' – a name which has stuck for almost two hundred years. (The Bank's quarterly house magazine is called *The Old Lady*.)

In 1844, when the Bank was formally given monopoly powers to make and issue banknotes, it began to assume the character of a central bank, despite its insistence that it must remain a public company. It not only issued notes, but took on responsibility for being the lender of last resort – the bank to which others turn in a crisis. One of those crises occurred in 1866, when the Overend Gurney collapse originated the doom-laden stock-exchange phrase 'Black Friday'. Again in 1890, and at the time of the Great Crash from 1929 to 1931, the Bank's policies in hard times were bitterly criticized, and one nineteenth-century Governor disgraced his office by dying scandalously in debt to the Bank, presumably having granted himself an overdraft. Though on each of these occasions the authority of the Bank was undermined, they did not prevent the Bank from becoming a metaphor for security and probity – 'as safe as the Bank of England'. No other bank could produce a jingle anything like it.

The passion for security is deliberate, since it helps foster the myth. The Bank's legendary impregnability is, as it were, a symbol of potency, and the security surrounding the bullion vaults three floors below Threadneedle Street is so intimidating that no robbers have ever tried a break-in. This is one of the three largest repositories of gold bullion in the world, and knowing officials in the Bank hint that it may contain even more gold than the other two, in Fort Knox and at the New York Federal Reserve Bank. Visitors are not allowed near the Bank's vaults, the theory being that even incidental intelligence might undermine security. It is, of course, part of the ballyhoo, but the system has proved faultless so far – except perhaps for one episode that is recorded in a book called *The Bank of England from Within*, written between the wars by a veteran Bank man named W. Marston Acres.

> The directors received an anonymous letter stating that the writer had means of access to their bullion room. They treated the matter as a hoax and took no notice of the letter. Another more urgent and more specific letter failed to rouse them. At length the writer offered to meet them in the bullion room at any hour they pleased to name. They then communicated with their correspondent through the channel he had indicated, appointing some 'dark and midnight hour' for the rendezvous. A deputation from the board, lantern in hand, repaired to the bullion room, locked themselves in, and awaited the arrival of the mysterious correspondent. Punctual to the hour, a noise was heard below. Some boards were without much trouble displaced, and in a few minutes the Guy Fawkes of the Bank stood in the midst of the astonished directors. His story was simple and straightforward. An old drain ran under the bullion room, the existence of which had become known to him, and by means of which he may have carried away enormous sums. Inquiry was made. Nothing had been abstracted, and the directors rewarded the honesty and ingenuity of their anonymous correspondent – a working man who had been employed in repairing the sewers – by a present of £800.

Acres believed the story to be true, and supports it with evidence of an anxious correspondence between the Bank architect and the City Commissioner of Sewers. On the other hand, there is no record of a payment of £800 to a working man of any kind, and the Bank keeps meticulous accounts of income and expenditure. Acres's tradition of internal inquiry was carried on by Derek Byatt, the Bank's chief bullion dealer until 1986, and while he concedes that the payment could have been hidden in the accounts, the fact that he can find no record at all of it leads him to doubt the truth of the story. But it does not really matter whether it is true: the tangle of history and myth helps heighten the sense of awe. If the alleged 'break-in' happened at all, it took place 150 years ago, in 1836. Somehow that makes the Bank appear even safer.

The tale of a picket of troops marching through the City each night to guard the Bank was once true, but since the soldiers were replaced by electronic surveillance in 1973 the picket has also become part of the myth. (Is it true or false, for example, that a Guards officer, caught after having smuggled a young woman into the Bank for purposes of pure pleasure, was told by his commanding officer to apologize to the directors of the Bank and replied: 'Apologize to a lot of tradesmen? I'll send in my papers first!')

The building on Threadneedle Street was specifically designed to sustain the idea of impregnability. The thirty-foot-high curtain stone wall that surrounds the Bank's three-acre site was the design of the distinguished Georgian architect, Sir John Soane, in response to the Gordon riots, which threatened the security of the Bank in 1780. Soane's exterior incorporated earlier buildings and was built around a number of courtyards. The rooms were high and light, and Sir Osbert Sitwell, who led the picket to the Bank in 1913, recalled a quiet, leafy, well-kept one-storey building whose garden courts and cloisters resembled a monastery on still evenings. Soane's entrance to Bullion Yard – inside the Bank's heavily guarded back door – was modelled on the triumphal arch of Constantine the Great in Rome.

The destruction of much of Soane's architectural jewel can be attributed in part to the growth of the national debt during the First World War. New bond holders had to be registered, more dividends paid, and extra staff were required; the option of housing them elsewhere seems not to have been considered. The architect chosen to rebuild the Bank was Sir Herbert Baker, who had done memorable work in New Delhi and South Africa, and who offered to design a building 'which might contain the elements of architectural dignity commensurate with the Bank's position and destiny in the City and the Empire'. The only obvious relic of Soane's bank is the curtain wall, and much of the site was buried under a new seven-storey office block completed in 1938. Although old Bank of England men dislike the

Baker building, almost to a man, it did meet with some critical enthusiasm ('an undertaking that deserves to rank with the building of the new Houses of Parliament as the greatest event which has taken place in the rebuilding of London in the last hundred years,' wrote Harold Clunn in 1951).

The Bank men who could recall the Soane buildings were members of the last generation to describe themselves with a straight face as 'gentlemen of the Bank of England'. Most of them had been to public school, and only a few had bothered to go on to university. The Bank was class-conscious and hierarchical. When Arthur Pointer left the Navy and joined the Bank in 1945 he was noticed hardly at all, and younger men were not expected to address their superiors until they had first been spoken to. Things were done a certain way because they had always been done that way, and clever people put up with the discomforts of junior status because the job was utterly secure and the fringe benefits were unusually attractive: $2\frac{1}{2}$ per cent mortgages and help with school fees. It was a proud and snobbish institution in which it was assumed that people from a similar background could be trusted to think alike. As late as 1967 an emissary was chosen to go to Australia to seek a favour from the Prime Minister because they had been at Oxford together. The premise was not mistaken; the favour was granted. A decade later, when a delegation from the Bank was to meet Sheikh Yamani, its members were briefed by the captain of the Bank's soccer team, since the Saudis were more concerned about Chelsea and Liverpool than Christ Church and Magdalen.

Attitudes inside the Bank began to change in the late 1970s, when job security could no longer be taken for granted, and later when the fringe benefits were taxed. Widespread fear of redundancy diminished the traditional loyalty from the staff to the Bank. Nor is privilege accepted as uncritically as it once was; the one issue that unites a group of younger Bank staff is the injustice of the fourth-floor dining-room being open only to the top fifty managers. It is known as the Golden Trough. The complaint is that – unlike their own meals – it is free. Not that the rest of the staff are ignored: they are members of a heavily subsidized club in an alleyway off Lothbury behind the Bank which drums up business by offering a Happy Hour at 5 p.m. on Fridays. (Business was so good at lunch times that the number of bar staff was cut to reduce the speed of consumption.) Old Bank men are horrified at the intrusion of such modern attitudes, but they are

overwhelmed numerically by new Bank men, one of whose character-
istics is that they rarely refer to themselves as Bank men at all,
especially if they are women. It may be the end of an era.

The offices from which the business of the Bank is now conducted
are grouped around two wells. One contains Bullion Yard and the
remnants of Soane's triumphal arch, and a grander one contains Garden
Court, which has fine green lawns and beds planted out with the
flowers grown in greenhouses at the sports ground in Roehampton.
Before I first visited the Bank I had heard that so little light penetrated
Garden Court that the Bank gave nature a helping hand by fixing
artificial lights. This seemed to parody the Bank's determination to
create the right image and I doubted the story, but it was true: artificial
light had been tried, but did not work. The reason why the grass looks
so green is that an enterprising gardener came across a new strain of
shade-loving grass seed.

In the past few years the Bank has spent less money on itself.
The concept of invulnerability was dented when the power station in
the basement was closed down. Water is still drawn from four wells
under the building, but power comes from the grid. Elderly messengers
observe that the odd discarded cigarette-end litters the floor – which
never used to be the case – but the maintenance staff has been halved
in less than a decade. None the less, the Bank is conspicuously better
kept than most buildings in London. On the ground floor the doors are
made of gleaming Cuban mahogany, and the walls are faced with
Derbyshire stone. The floors make compulsive viewing, for they contain
the illustrated history in mosaic of the British currency from William
the Conqueror to George V. It is particularly difficult not to linger at
the junction that leads to the directors' offices, where a mosaic of the
two-headed god Janus bears the unmistakable profile of Montagu
Norman, the Governor from 1920 to 1944. Norman did not like this
ambiguous portrayal. He was even less pleased by the portrait of him
by Augustus John that hangs outside the Courtroom and shows an
elderly and supercilious figure.

The Courtroom is perfectly proportioned, with decorative plaster-
work on the ceiling well lit by fine chandeliers, and gilded profiles
along the wall of earlier monarchs in the Bank's history, from William
III to Queen Victoria. (The present room, which was moved intact
from the ground to the first floor when Baker rebuilt the Bank, is itself
a replica of an earlier Courtroom.) The chairs around the imposing

table at which the Court sits are Sheraton in style, and there is an original Sheraton table on one side of the Adam fireplace. On the other side is a perfect reproduction of this table, made by one of the cabinet-makers on the Bank's staff. By the wall is the writing-table belonging to William Pitt, Prime Minister during the Napoleonic Wars. A wind dial is visible from each seat of the table, and dates from 1805, when the Court was anxious to know whether there were strong easterly winds to bring the East India Company's bullion ships into the Port of London. The paintings are eighteenth-century London scenes by the Irish painter, H. Pugh. I once remarked to a Bank man who was showing me the room that it was a pity not to have a Canaletto of the same period. 'We have,' he replied, 'but we're not sure it's authentic.'

The eminent Victorian economic journalist, Walter Bagehot, who was especially shrewd about the Bank, commented on the youthfulness of some of the directors in his day. He was surprised to find them fresh, cheerful and nice-looking gentlemen, most of whom would eventually become Governor, because in those days his term was limited to two years. The directors were men of power, who fixed the bank rate – the guide to the prevailing interest rate on borrowed money. The transfer of power away from the directors began with Norman's twenty-five-year term. More seeped away in 1946 when the Labour government nationalized the Bank, and the collective power of the Court effectively ceased in 1957 when one of the directors was accused of having bene-fited from a premature leak of a change in bank rate. It was a scandal, and the ensuing tribunal of inquiry recommended that the Bank's secrets should no longer be shared with the Court.

Arriving for their Thursday meetings, directors of the Bank of England are still met by the head gatekeeper wearing a deep red velvet robe and a black tricorn hat, and carrying an eighteenth-century silver-topped staff, all part of the mystique known as keeping up appearances. Being a non-executive director of the Bank (there are a dozen of them) provides useful access to incidental economic intelligence and some prestige, but power resides elsewhere, in the rooms known as the Parlours a floor below the Courtroom.

The knobs on the doors leading to the Parlours are designed to confuse a stranger since they do not turn. The door is opened by pressing a concealed button in the knob and leads on to a long corridor carpeted in pale pink, which nicely sets off the polished wooden hatstands and the side-tables. The Parlours are a set of large, com-

fortable offices that overlook Garden Court, and they are watched over
by the parlour stewards, also dressed in red and pink, who manage to
be simultaneously deferential and imposing. Voices in the corridor
always seem to be lowered and there are junior members of the staff
who believe it is still necessary to enter the Parlours by the door at one
end of the corridor, and leave by the door at the other end. They are
not sure why.

On the dark side of the corridor are a number of small waiting-
rooms (numerous enough so that one director's visitors need not be
seen by another's), each with a desk, a chair, and a copy of *Country
Life*. (The Bank is an ideal place to study the rural property market.)
Across the corridor are the offices of the members of the Court of
the Bank, the permanent or executive directors and the associates,
the deputy governor and the Governor himself. They are spacious
rooms, with high ceilings, marble fireplaces, good portraits and prints
on the walls, and in each of them is the sound of a clock ticking. A
quick tour of the Parlours in the summer of 1986 revealed who did
what at the top of the Bank's hierarchy (and shows how it still works).

Starting at the far end of the corridor on the east side of Garden
Court: this is the office of the economic advisor to the Governor, John
Flemming, who notes the significance of the Bank's geography. His
own department is situated three floors away, and there is no way that
one of his economists can poke his head round the door for an idle chat
about the Medium-term Financial Strategy. 'The Bank inhibits speech,
partly for reasons of geography,' he says. Flemming is mildly profes-
sorial (he was an Oxford professor, after all) and speaks of the virtues
of collegiality rather than doctrine, though this view did not prevail
among the Bank's economists when Flemming arrived in the early
1980s and there was still doctrinal ferment about varieties of monetarism. This argument was conducted by two men who have since left
the Bank, Christopher Dow and Charles Goodhart, one a neo-
Keynesian, the other a neo-monetarist. Under Flemming the economic
department is less agitated and more functional. It is also less influential: 'Economists are at a discount in the Bank at the moment,' says
one director.

Rodney Galpin occupied the next office in September 1985, having been promoted to executive director and put in charge of bank
supervision. This signalled the letting of blood in the Parlours as a
result of the bail-out of Johnson Matthey Bankers. Galpin is one of the

24

remaining old Bank men, easy to identify because his photograph appears in the history of the Sports Club as a member of the Extra A rugby team in 1952. He is instantly recognizable – tall, with the same trim moustache and slicked-back hair. The only thing the photograph does not show is the smile. On the wall there is an Augustus John portrait of Lord Cunliffe, one of the nastiest men ever to be Governor. He fought the Treasury during the First World War and was once described (by an old Bank man) as 'a real pig for England'. The portraits in these offices sometimes provide a clue to the personality of the occupant, and the presence of Lord Cunliffe may signify that Galpin is not as nice as he looks; after the failure of JMB that may also be a qualification for the post.

His predecessor as the head of banking supervision was Peter Cooke, and although he retains an office in the Parlours, his responsibilities have shrunk. He is, however, chairman of the committee of bank supervisors from the world's leading economies that meets in Basle and bears his name. It was Cooke's blood that was shed in the Parlours, but it was cleaned up so expeditiously that only insiders really noticed.

Galpin was previously an associate director in charge of operations and services, a catch-all title which gave one man ultimate responsibility for virtually everything in the Bank that did not involve policy-making. It allows the old Bank man who normally has the job to take a detached view of the way the place works. The present incumbent is Douglas Dawkins, who has worked in the Bank since 1950 and was the head of the exchange control department when it summarily ceased to exist in 1979. On the day we met he said that he had just seen the first male recruit to wear an earring. In the 1950s, he said, he would have been sent home for wearing a pair of suede shoes, but what interested him about the earring was that a job at the Bank was attractive to the man who wore it and, second, that no one had thought to tell him to remove it. That would have been poor personnel management, a concept that the Bank has taken seriously for some time now. Dawkins declared that the Bank might eventually draw the line, but only at a safety-pin through the nose. In earlier days, the main qualification of a memorable holder of the post of personnel director was that while at Cambridge he had bowled Don Bradman.

The distinction within the Bank that concerns Dawkins has nothing to do with class or schooling. It is the gap that exists between

25

the policy divisions, like banking supervision, for example, and the rest of the Bank. Dawkins is committed to ridding the Bank of the distinction, but as time goes by his task grows ever more difficult, because élites are becoming more, not less, entrenched.

Until 1980 the desirable suite of offices on the west side of Garden Court had its own entrance and was occupied by the chief cashier and his senior staff in the banking department. The Bank had been divided roughly into thinkers and doers, and the chief cashier was the man who got things done. He was chairman of the committee of departmental heads that effectively ran the Bank until 1980, when Gordon Richardson simply erased the post of chief cashier from the power structure, kicking the office-holder upstairs – literally – to the third floor. The present holder of the post is David Somerset – his name still appears on banknotes – who is subordinate to Rodney Galpin.

The chief cashier's suite was colonized by the monetary-policy division which deals directly with the money and gilt-edged markets and occupies the front line in the Bank's relationship with the Treasury. Its director is Edward George (known as Eddie or E.A.I.G.), a stocky figure with thinning hair and rimless spectacles, and his group immodestly considers itself to be the *crème de la crème*. They pride themselves on doing and thinking, and the atmosphere in George's office is different from the others around Garden Court. There is no clock, since the screens flashing late market information always tell him the time. There are no paintings on the walls, only a replica of the announcement of a government bond issue. George's confidence and status is reflected in what colleagues say about him. (An Australian central banker stays an extra day in London if that is the only way he can see George: 'Always worth it,' he remarks.)

The élite was not always to be found in George's department. In the 1970s the economists were briefly pre-eminent, and before that, when exchange rates were fixed and sterling needed stout defenders, it was the overseas department that absorbed a high proportion of the Bright Young Men. Anthony Loehnis, executive director of the overseas division, has one of the offices on the south side of the Court which gets the mid-morning sun. He was hired by Richardson, having earlier left the Foreign Office for Schroders Bank, but when he became executive director of the division, in 1981, there was already rather less for it to do than when it was run by Sir Kit McMahon in the 1970s. A majority of the graduates recruited by the Bank used to go into the overseas division, but now most go into banking supervision. Loehnis says defiantly that he was not brought in to do a hatchet job on the international side of the Bank's activities. 'We have a tradition, and it does a lot for the reputation of the Bank,' he says. Maybe, but some of his staff do appear sorry for themselves.

Only one director does not have an office in the Parlours. David Walker never moved down from the third floor when he was promoted, and he has his own pink-coated steward in a suite of offices reached by a lift that can be operated only by himself, his steward, and a select number of senior staff to whom he has awarded a key. Walker's remit is finance and industry, an omnibus title. 'He abhors a vacuum,' says a colleague, who has watched Walker involve himself in virtually all the City's recent preoccupations – restrictive practices at the Stock Exchange, fraud at Lloyds, the collapse of the tin market and the regulation of the securities industry. He strides unstoppably through the corridors near his office like a ship under full sail; and junior members of his staff like to believe that the reason he does not have an office in the Parlours is so that he can shout at them, personally. Richardson spotted him in the Treasury, where he was unlike most civil servants, and when he came to the Bank it was clear that he was unlike most central bankers. He lacks their patience and prudence, and they call him Walker the Talker.

Every Thursday morning at 9 a.m. the executive and associate directors gather for the deputy governor's meeting in the first-floor committee room, complete with clock and fireplace. The group was formed when Kit McMahon was deputy governor and has effectively taken the place of the heads of department meeting which was once chaired by the chief cashier. It has become an executive committee, discussing policy, especially bank supervision. All the directors except Dawkins, who leaves the meeting at half-time, have a supervisory role of one kind or another.

George Blunden is deputy governor, and the only reason he is at the Bank at all is the failure of supervision in the Johnson Matthey Bank case. Having worked at the Bank all his life, like his father before him, Blunden retired as an executive director on 28 February 1984, and was immediately appointed a non-executive director, only to return to the Bank full-time on 1 January 1986 when Kit McMahon resigned to become chief executive of the Midland Bank. Downing Street opted for a tough old professional rather than one of the clever

27

young men like Walker or George, and Blunden, who had experience of bank supervision during the 1970s, relishes his role. I once described him as 'a silver-haired and avuncular man'. He does, indeed, have a full head of silver hair, but it was clear when we met again that he was mildly amused by the idea that he might be avuncular. After spending more time at the Bank I discovered Blunden's reputation for astringency. He is, in fact, a somewhat old-fashioned disciplinarian who is impatient with junior staff who do not meet his high expectations. He makes a suitable foil for the Governor, Robin Leigh-Pemberton.

The Governor's room is the largest in the Parlours, with two fireplaces and two clocks, giving the impression of a stereophonic tick-tock. Leigh-Pemberton sits at the side of a leather-topped table on an upholstered chair that was built for comfort rather than style, and on the desk in front of him are a silver inkstand, and a silver bell, to call for service, presumably. A line of chairs is set out before the Governor's desk, and each morning at 11 a.m. the deputy governor, the executive directors and a number of senior officials join him for the meeting known as 'Books', which has its origins in the days when the Governor and the chief cashier looked at the balance-sheet – the books of account. The Governor sits behind his desk facing the horseshoe of chairs on which the Bank's senior officials sit, with their papers perched on their knees. One of the skills of central banking in London is to prevent these papers spilling on to the floor. A generation ago the chief cashier still concentrated on the books, even to the point of naming members of the staff who had overdrawn their accounts at the Bank. Now Books is a means by which departmental heads explain the trends in monetary or funding policy. First to report is the head of the money-markets division, who describes market behaviour the previous day and explains his tactics for the rest of the day. Next the head of the gilt-edged division outlines factors that will influence the market, and the head of the foreign-exchange division talks about the previous twenty-four hours in the markets. The money-markets men like to concentrate on the facts and do not greatly encourage conversation about their activities, and on days when their reticence prevails, Books is over in five minutes. But when conversation opens up and develops as it goes down the row of senior officials, each taking their turn to speak, it can last for forty-five minutes. Philip Warland, head of the information department, observes: 'It can be very funny at times, for a number of senior people have a well-developed sense of humour.

Equally, there is a reaction if one is too blatant in criticizing another's operations. Everyone understands how the game is played, and both the Governor and the deputy pounce like hawks when they feel they are less well informed than they ought to be. Sometimes they raise issues which it is clear that the officials involved would prefer to keep to themselves. It keeps senior people in touch with everything the Bank is doing, and even when issues are kept so close that they are not brought out in Books you can usually sense a particular tension, and go and probe afterwards and find out what is going on.'

Being Governor of the Bank is a shapeless sort of job. In an attempt to make sense of it, successive Governors, including Leigh-Pemberton, have reaffirmed the belief that they are custodians of the nation's money. This is a largely mythic obligation since if it really were the responsibility of the Governor to preserve the value of Britain's money all recent occupants of the post would first have been ridiculed and then impeached and finally deported to a cold climate instead of being appointed Privy Councillors and ennobled on their retirement. The idea of guarding the nation's money is suggestive of order and stability, and as such it is an idyll conjured up by central bankers. In real life the money they are custodians of has fallen in value so fast that one pound today buys 10 pence worth of goods at 1950 prices. So the job is something else, and definitions of it change according to the character of the Governor.

A Governor exercises authority, but where and how depends on who he is. Some Governors concentrate on their natural constituency in the City, and have been content to deploy their power among people who are close enough to notice when they raise their eyebrows in an expression of displeasure. Others wish to extend their power to Westminster and Whitehall and, by playing a role in the development of economic policy, have a direct influence on it. Some Governors, like Gordon Richardson, are governors, and others, like Robin Leigh-Pemberton, are like chairmen of the board.

Richardson was slow to reach conclusions. In his era ideas were picked apart and put together again gradually while a consensus developed. Leigh-Pemberton tends to say 'yes' or 'no' to an idea. He delegates authority and is generous with his praise. When he became Governor, his experience of central banking was non-existent. Clearly he is a conspicuously decent man and a good manager, but central bankers did question whether these qualifications were sufficient, for the characteristic they most admire in the central bank is independence. In Germany the independence of the Bundesbank is enshrined in the constitution. In the United States the freedom of the Federal Reserve System to implement monetary policy is written into the law. In London the Governor of the Bank of England has to rely on the history, experience and expertise of the Bank.

Before 1946, when the Bank still had shareholders, it was jealous of its independence, even though it was as susceptible to influence as any other bank with one major client would be. Montagu Norman wooed the Chancellor, calling on the Treasury regularly on his way home to Camden Hill, and for three decades after the Second World War the Bank behaved as though nationalization in 1946 had changed hardly anything. For some years in the 1960s it resisted inquiry by the House of Commons select committee on nationalized industries, and acted as though its dignity were affronted if its independence were questioned. (The Bank complained to the Federal Reserve Board's international department when an American magazine listed the Bank among those central banks that are not independent of government.)

The Bank argues the case for its independence as follows: the City of London requires a sympathetic broker to explain it to the government, and, in turn, Whitehall needs an intermediary to make sense of its policies in the City. This pivotal role can only be fulfilled effectively, so the argument goes, when the Bank is trusted by each side. Therefore it must be independent of both. This case has some theoretical substance, but another factor is more important in practice. Walter Bagehot was crisply realistic about it. Writing in 1873 about the balance of power between the Bank and the government, he said: 'I confess that I believe this varies very much with the character of the Governor for the time being. A strong Governor does much mainly on his own responsibility, and a weak Governor does little.'

It is not fashionable among economists, who often prefer statistical models, or among central bankers, who find the idea of celebrity instinctively distasteful, to attribute the power of a central bank to the personality of its chairman or governor. If nothing else, this undermines the idea of institutional continuity and stability. But there is much evidence to support the idea (consider Paul Volcker in Washington, Otmar Emminger and Karl Otto Poehl in Frankfurt, Jelle Zijlstra in The Hague and Fritz Leutwiler in Basle). Doing the top job well is much like being a great actor-manager, satisfying both the company he leads and the audience he plays to. Like all the best performances, it is difficult to know exactly how it is done, but instantly recognizable when it is done well. Before making any critical judgements about the style, the independence and the authority of the Bank of England, however, it is as well to acquaint ourselves with exactly what it is there for, what it does and how it is done.

2

The Nation's Money

Central banking is really quite straightforward. The Bank of England first manufactures the basic product, which is paper money that comes in four different sizes and colours. Next, the Bank helps to set the price for the money; it sells a great deal of the money; and finally it distributes the money to the consumers.

These jobs are performed on Bank premises and while they may sound simple, the practices are arcane. Until a decade or so ago the Bank protected these activities from the public gaze. Its confidential relationship with the Treasury and the requirements of security were the reasons given. Now that the Bank has been largely cured of that habit, it is possible to understand its job by watching it happen. Even so, to make sense of the Bank's work it is necessary to be very clear about what it is trying to achieve.

Early in the morning and late at night the Bank's concern is to ensure that the books of the British banking system are balanced. The reason the Bank performs this role is that the largest single element in the system is the government – collecting taxes and paying its bills – and, as the government's banker, the Bank takes the strain. One day late in 1986, it happened like this:

It is 9.20 a.m. in the banking department, and the Treasury appears to have lost £100 million. 'Oh knickers,' says the manager as he pores over the specially designed paper pad on which he writes the banking system's income and expenditure for the previous day. A call on the direct line to the Treasury accounting office has failed to explain the missing £100 million, and the sums on the page are being done and redone, figures pencilled in, and others rubbed out. In the electronic age, the method appears unscientific. 'It's much better to talk to these figures than to have them cold on the screen,' says the manager, who is swearing at them this morning, since he really ought to be getting on and preparing a rough balance for the day's activities. (Incidentally, the Treasury later discovers that the Paymaster General forgot to report an additional £100 million paid in tax the previous day.)

Each morning the Treasury tells the Bank how much it expects to receive from individual citizens and companies paying taxes and what it expects to spend; since the government normally receives more than it pays out, the British commercial banks usually anticipate being short of money at the beginning of the day, and their balances look as if they will be in the red. This debit balance is known as the shortage, and when the man in the banking department has done his calculations a message goes out to the money markets via the Reuter information screens. This morning it appears at 9.56 a.m., and reads: 'Money-market operations. Official Bank of England input, morning forecast. A shortage of around stg 150mn is expected today.'

The sum is arrived at by deducting the sum paid out by the Treasury to meet items like social-security payments and defence contractors' bills, from the sum drawn in by the Treasury, made up mainly of the money required to redeem Treasury bills that are due for repayment. This rough calculation, on this day, shows that the clearing banks – the high-street banks, NatWest, Midland, Lloyds and Barclays, and smaller institutions like the Scottish clearers and Standard Chartered – will pay out about £150 million more than they take in and to balance their books by the end of the day (to the nearest £10 million or so) they need to borrow. They do this at discount houses in the City of London, and if the discount houses do not have enough to lend they, in turn, borrow from the Bank of England.

Later in the morning the shortage rises. At 10.15 a.m. it is £257 million, and shortly before midday, when the clearing banks and the discount houses have made their own calculations of the day's shortage, it has risen to £400 million. By now the money-market division of the Bank has contacted the discount houses to discover how much money they have available to supply to the clearers and how much the clearers will demand. Often the discount houses prefer to keep the Bank guessing, but this morning they are nervous and they want to ensure the supply – from the Bank – at the first opportunity. The money-market specialist reports to the assistant director of the money-market division that the discount houses foresee a shortage of £330 million. To find this money the discount houses need to sell short-term securities – mainly commercial bills – to the Bank. They offer £296.6 million, at the prevailing rate of interest. 'Take the lot,' says the assistant director, because the price is right. 'Rather satisfactory,' he says, looking up from the telephone speaker that connects him with the dealing room.

When the next calculation of the shortage is made at 2 p.m., it has fallen back from £400 million to £300 million – less than the sum that the discount houses have already raised. The active business of the money-market division is over for the day and the clearing banks' books will now balance. In the banking department, however, work has just begun again after a lull. The discount houses, having sold roughly £300 million in bills, have to send them to Threadneedle Street in bundles of bills – Treasury bills or commercial bills – which are like post-dated cheques that have been discounted. (For instance, a coffee importer buys 200 bags of coffee, but his cheque for £80,000 is dated three months hence, so it is sold to a discount house for £77,500.)

Meanwhile the manager in the banking department who had trouble with the Treasury that morning has his pencil, a rubber and his special pad to work out exactly the shortage in the day's banking operations. Though his day started at 8.50 a.m. with an estimated shortage of £150 million, which has become £300 million by 4.30 p.m., the margin of error is perfectly acceptable and the day has been un-remarkable. This is not always the case. Sometimes the circulation of money in the system is sluggish and by 2.45 p.m. the discount houses have not obtained enough money to lend on to the banks. In that case, representatives from the discount houses call personally on the Bank and ask to borrow enough money to balance their books. The discussion takes place in shorthand behind closed doors and sounds something like this: 'Bob, I can do six overnight at twelve and a quarter and 90 at three quarters till Monday.' It is the price the discount houses pay to balance their books, and it is an example of the Bank of England's acting as lender of last resort, because by that time of day the discount houses have nowhere else to go.

Helping banks to balance their books seems, on the face of it, to be a neutral activity, but the procedure can also be used to enable the Bank to fulfil a second function. Although the rate of interest, known for decades as bank rate, is no longer formally announced after the Thursday meeting of the Court, the Bank is still expected to use its influence in the market to steady the rate of interest and keep it where the Chancellor and the Governor have privately agreed it ought to be. To do this the Bank must sometimes steer the market. Like this:

At 10.15 a.m., shortly after the extent of the shortage has gone out on the Reuter screens, the money-market division holds its morning meeting in the panelled office of the assistant director, money markets, overlooking Garden Court. He sits on one side of a large leather-topped partners' desk, flanked by three screens reporting the latest market information. Opposite him sits Eddie George, the division's executive director, and round the room in upright chairs are the specialists who concentrate on various segments of the money markets. Some then stay in the Bank watching screens and talking on the telephone: others put on top hats and do the rounds of the City. At the morning meeting they drink coffee and swap information about the state of the market in terms that are easy and egalitarian.

This morning the news is that one of the discount houses is offering to buy bills in the market at $\frac{1}{32}$ per cent over the prevailing interest rate. This reveals that the market is already nervous; if more discount houses follow suit, the market will become more nervous, and there will be a strong expectation of a rise in the interest rates. If the Treasury had no objection to a rise in interest rates, the Bank would do nothing. But on this morning the policy is to keep the rates where they are, so the upward pressure on the rate must be resisted.

Money-supply figures are to be released later in the day and, showing a large jump as they do, are a cause for some anxiety. George briefly outlines the Bank's response. The message going out of the dealing room, and in the offices of market participants, ought to stress that last month's figures were not so bad: 'Encourage them to look at the two months together,' says George. The idea is to calm the market.

At 10.25 Malcolm Gill, the head of the foreign-exchange division, slips into the room carrying the large pad of cream paper on which changes in the values of all the leading currencies are pencilled in. (A computer screen can state the price at any one moment but does not reveal the pattern of price changes during the day.) 'What's cable?' Gill is asked. 'Cable' is the market jargon for sterling, and the news is that it is a bit soggy in the Far East. An opinion poll showing Labour leading the Tories brings the price down in Tokyo and Hong Kong, and is most unhelpful; when sterling falls, markets expect interest rates to rise. George says that the Chancellor is scheduled to appear before a Commons select committee that afternoon and will say that the Treasury thinks the exchange rate has fallen enough. Gill reports that despite its bad start in the east, sterling did recover when the London market opened that morning.

GEORGE: You're not spending anything at the moment?
GILL: No.
GEORGE: No point in getting behind it?
GILL: A fifty million order filled slowly just now. There doesn't seem to be any point.

This is the language George uses to discuss whether the Bank ought to intervene in foreign-exchange markets. To keep up the sterling price, George would have suggested that Gill use government funds to

37

buy pounds, in the hope that it would relieve the pressure on the rate of interest.

The next moment at which the Bank can intervene is at midday, when the discount houses borrow from the Bank to end the shortage. Since the rate of interest in the market reflects the availability of money, when the Bank wants the interest rate to stay steady it will meet the demands of the discount houses without bothering to bargain. This morning the assistant director of the money-market division was happy to lend as much as the discount houses asked for. If the Bank had wanted interest rates to rise he would have created a scarcity by buying less than the £296.6 million from the discount houses, forcing them to offer to borrow more – at a higher rate of interest.

A third function of the Bank is to borrow money for the government. Because British governments are not expected to default on their loans, these are gilt-edged, and there is a large market for them. As the seller of these gilt-edged bonds, the Bank is in a position to influence the price they are bought and sold for in the market, and that price is another way of expressing the rate of interest. There was an indication of this in the morning meeting.

The government broker, the Bank's chief trader in the market, enters the room and stands at George's side. 'Good morning, government broker, you're looking sick today,' says George. 'Shorts are one eighth off, mediums and longs one quarter off,' reports the government broker. His colleague Ian Plenderleith, the assistant director in charge of the gilts division, produces a graph from his folder which shows how gilt prices have fallen in the past few days, another indication that interest rates are pushing up.

Before Big Bang the government broker worked for a company called Mullens and acted as the Bank's agent in the securities market. But Mullens was sold, the market was opened to a large number of new players, and it no longer made sense for the Bank to remain aloof from the market. Behaving like principals in the market meant adopting their methods, and it was impossible to do this without a dealing room. The one that was constructed is quite different from any other room in the building. The banking department, for instance, is in a spacious hall three storeys high filled with natural light. The dealing room looks as though it was made out of a hole in the ground. There are no windows, and strip lighting in a low ceiling illuminates a long table with five dealers seated down both sides each looking at a battery of three screens. The colour scheme is dominated by shades of grey and brown, and the walls are decorated only by clocks showing the time in London, New York and Tokyo. The technology, on the other hand, is just as smart as it can be.

Each dealer has a keyboard which gives him access to the information that can be summoned up on the screens in front of him (and her, for there are two women dealers). Another screen built into the desk by the keyboard is an individual telephone exchange, showing the names and numbers of all the major gilt-edged dealers. When a Bank dealer wants to speak to Merrill Lynch, for example, he presses his finger on the heat-sensitive glass over the name of Merrill Lynch on the screen and he is put through automatically. (The interruption of two light beams triggers the call, so they say.) Incoming calls do not ring; they flash up on the screen. The telephone receiver lies on the desk top to the dealer's left. On his right is a built-in calculator, and a socket designed for a plastic cup. (No china in the dealing room; no pink-coated men to serve the tea.)

John Hill, the chief gilts dealer, arrives at 8 a.m. to read the papers and check for overnight activity in markets that affect government bond prices – oil, foreign exchange, the money markets in London and New York, and the futures market in Chicago – and by 8.30 he starts telephoning dealers round the City. By 9 a.m. he is talking to Ian Plenderleith to discuss the day's tactics.

This morning, as we have seen, gilt prices are falling because market analysts expect interest rates to rise, so Hill and Plenderleith agree not to sell any bonds at all for the time being, creating a shortage that might drive prices up. Hill passes the message to the dealers at 9.20 a.m. The telephone flashes and a City broker makes a bid for a Treasury bond issue. The dealer replies that he cannot help. The price is not good enough, not close, try again, he says. The Bank's dealer will show no interest until the bids are in line with the interest rate the Bank is determined to preserve – at any rate, until the Bank is forced to submit to market pressure.

The game is not always like cat and mouse. At other times, when it wishes to sell a new issue to dealers who already have too many government bonds on their books, the Bank may buy some stock back from the dealer to leave him free to take some of the new issue. When the Bank enters the market it is like other players, winning on some deals and losing on others, though victory and defeat are not calculated in normal market terms. 'Market management and government policy are paramount; profit is secondary,' says Hill.

There is no profit-and-loss account in the Bank's other dealing room, which is well lit and well established. This is the foreign-exchange dealing room, where winning and losing are defined by yet another set of standards. This was once one of the engine rooms of the Bank, where speculative attacks on sterling were fought off, and fixed exchange rates defended (remember $2.40 to £1?). Eddie George and Malcolm Gill still consider tactical purchases in the market as they did at this morning's meeting, but the deployment of billions of pounds from the reserves to buy sterling in the hope of supporting the price is no longer part of the armoury. 'Intervention nowadays is like walking into the middle of the M1 and trying to stop the traffic by putting up your hand,' says Graham Cocks, the chief foreign-exchange dealer. He can hold the value of the pound steady for a day, he says, but that is all.

Cocks runs the Bank's intelligence operation in the foreign-exchange markets, listening to the fevered exchanges among dealers and reporting on trends and developments. And much of the time he is one of them, because Cocks is a participant in the market as manager of the government's foreign-exchange reserves. He buys currency for, say, the Ministry of Defence, and acts as a dealer on behalf of other, smaller central banks. He judges himself by the standards of other dealers, and, like all skilled operators in the City, considers his own dealing room the best at what it does. 'I can sniff the market better than anybody,' he says (meaning that he anticipates price movements as well as other dealers). But only for ten minutes; for any more protracted operation he consults Malcolm Gill, and if policy is involved Gill himself takes advice. 'The Treasury has the final say,' notes Cocks.

Of course it does. The central bank is the Treasury's agent. Daily tactics are settled at the Bank, but the strategy is worked out in a series of steps, first inside the Bank, and then in consultation with Treasury officials and ministers in Whitehall. (The Bank does business at the Treasury, and the Governor arrives in a Rolls-Royce; the Treasury generally calls on the Bank at lunch time.) At each level of the hierarchies in Threadneedle Street and Whitehall each Bank official has a counterpart in the Treasury, with whom policy is discussed continuously.

There are also formal monthly meetings, like the funding meeting, chaired by the financial secretary to the Treasury, at which decisions are taken about how to raise money for the government: how much is to be done through National Savings, and whether the bonds should be short term or long term, or indexed or not. A window was opened on these meetings by Jock Bruce-Gardyne, who was economic secretary between 1981 and 1983; in his book *Ministers and Mandarins*, he writes:

> The funding meetings simply applied what Whitehall likes to call an 'overview'. The actual course of funding and the choice of instruments appropriate for the purpose, were the subject of regular discussions between the Treasury and the Bank . . . There would be a submission from the Treasury, and a submission from the Bank. Usually they reached the same conclusion, the product of long hours of skilled negotiations. If so, the course was clear.
>
> Once or twice, greatly daring, I ventured to suggest that we might do something else. I was spitting in the wind. But occasionally life became more interesting. The officials had failed to reach an agreement. My duty was clear. It was to back the Treasury. On rare occasions I dared do the opposite. This was received with dismay. The officials would go back into another huddle and contrive to come up with a mutually acceptable solution – which I would reject at my peril.

Bruce-Gardyne describes bureaucratic politics, in which power is not something that can be defined by drawing a chart or plotting an organization's hierarchy. The relationship between the Treasury and the Bank reflects the authority of the Bank and therefore depends on personality. If the Governor is an intimate of the Chancellor, the Bank has an influence on broad macro-economic policy. When the Chancellor is not much interested in what the Governor thinks, the Governor spends more time talking to the permanent secretary of the Treasury, and the Bank's influence is diminished. The same pattern is repeated down the hierarchy: when the director of the money-markets division is respected for his technical skill, the Treasury is more inclined to delegate responsibility for the management of the government debt. The less confidence it has in the Bank, the more the Treasury interferes. The degree of independence permitted to the Bank is like the trade cycle: it goes up and down.

Compared to pricing money, or selling it, making money is wonderfully uncomplicated. On the face of it, this is just another printing process, and the five-pound notes roll off the press in a continuous stream at a rate of 3,650 a minute, just like newspapers, except that each of those 3,650 notes has a different number printed on it, twice, and each is made of paper that is so unusual that it is locked up at night. If a piece goes missing a security disaster is declared. This special paper is made of old rags and raw cotton, pulped at the Overton Mill near Whitchurch in Hampshire until it turns into a liquid with the consistency of porridge. The mill belongs to Portals, and 30 per cent of Portals belongs to the Bank of England, which is unwilling to take for granted the volume and quality of supply even though its customer relationship goes back well over a century. (Portals were trusted to make the paper for the crisp white banknotes with shaded watermarks that were introduced in 1855 and stayed in circulation for 102 years.) The cotton base makes the paper strong as well as creating the familiar smooth feel, and it is dense enough to absorb the watermark – which now looks three-dimensional – and the fine metal thread that runs through each note (or on it, in the case of the fifty-pound notes). But the object of putting so much effort into making the paper is not to provide tactile pleasure for the user, but to make it prodigiously difficult to duplicate.

Having been turned from pulp into paper, it is taken by road to Debden in Essex in tight reels containing two miles of paper for the fives and tens and in sheets for the twenties and fifties; there it is allowed to mature for two months, after which it absorbs the ink better. At Debden this plain white paper is counted, shut in cages of thick wire mesh, and stored behind locked gates, day and night. 'It's the paper that gives the forger the most difficulty,' says Geoffrey Wheatley, the head, until 1986, of the Bank's printing works, which was specially built in 1956 on a fifteen-acre site on the outskirts of London.

Notes were printed in Threadneedle Street until 1921, when a lunatic asylum in Old Street called St Luke's was converted into a printing works. It was here that the Bank's first green pound notes and rust-coloured ten-shilling notes were produced in 1928, and they satisfied a peculiarly British demand for small-denomination notes that has never really changed. The central banks of Germany, Italy, Spain and France each produce between 700 and 800 million notes a year, while Debden's output is 1,200 million a year, even after the disappearance of the pound note. At peak production in the 1970s close to two billion notes were produced every year (demand first fell when the government insisted on saving money by making notes last longer), and the difference in output was attributable entirely to the taste for fivers and tenners rather than notes worth fifty pounds and more. Wheatley is confident that the fifty is the highest denomination the works will ever be asked to produce.

Pressure of demand after the Second World War was one reason for the move to Debden. Security was the other. The watchtowers that are built into the structure can be seen from the M11. Originally, the idea was to make the site entirely secure without making it look like a prison, so that it might also be a pleasant place for printers to work. Today there are different priorities. The factory where money is made is a wonderfully tempting target for terrorist groups, and to deter them the perimeter fence is now topped by tight rolls of the vicious barbed wire that was first used in Ulster and which later became familiar at Rupert Murdoch's printing plant at Wapping. There is a neatly kept rose garden at the front entrance and no fewer than thirty acres of sports grounds.

Getting past the guards is an arduous process, and getting about inside is also very slow, since most doors are locked and visitors have to be individually identified before they get on to the factory floor. This is large (800 feet by 125 feet), noisy and underused, for there is a great deal of empty floor space. This is because there are no more pound notes. The last one-pound note was printed on 29 November 1984 and the loss of the pound business to Llantrisant, where all pound coins are produced by the Royal Mint, meant a cut of one third in the number of notes produced at Debden, and three hundred staff were made redundant. Portals were upset and the management of the printing works seethed: 'My own views were made clear, but in the end we do what the government wants,' says Wheatley.

The efficiency of the web machinery transforms bank-note printing from a manual operation on a letterpress machine into a mass-production engineering job. Six great machines produce ten million notes a day; the machines are manufactured by Molins, a company whose expertise was developed by printing cigarette cards, although the note-printing machines were developed by a company called Thrissell Ltd, which is jointly owned by Molins and the Bank of England. In fact, the enthusiasm of the management of the printing works for the further development and international sale of these machines is a cause of some embarrassment in Threadneedle Street, where trade is a matter of policy, not practice. But the management at

Debden talk like people from manufacturing industry rather than banking, and regard salary levels in the City with disquiet.

The letterpress machines still rattle as they impress the design of the notes on the paper – the process known as intaglio. The sound of the web machines is a relentless drone. Production is a monotonous business and even the trick of marking each note with a different number is made to sound prosaic: just like a pedometer on a bicycle apparently. The eye lingers only to watch the trays of ink, the consistency of double cream, in delicate shades of rich brown, red and blue. There are five pigments and twenty different shades of colour in a fiver, and the inks are all made on the premises, like the plates and the engravings from which the plates are made. Anywhere else might be insecure.

If Wheatley is correct and no denomination higher than the fifty-pound note is called for, the basic design for British banknotes will all have been done by a team of designers led by one man, named Harry Eccleston, who retired from the Bank in 1983. Eccleston, a small man with lush grey sideburns, worked in an artist's smock as befitted a man who was president of the Royal Society of Painters, Etchers and Engravers. His last job for the Bank was designing the master plate for the fifty-pound note, celebrating Christopher Wren, though the last pound notes featuring Sir Isaac Newton were his best-known work. (After the note had gone to press, Eccleston discovered an error in the geometric design from Newton's *Principia* which overlaid an illustration of the solar system. The edition from which he had copied it contained the error. He was mortified.)

The engraver's objective is to design notes that can be mass-produced to a consistently high quality inside the works, and not be reproduced outside it. Keeping ahead of the forgers means that each new note issue is more complex than its predecessors, with increasingly subtle variations of tone and colour. Amendments to Eccleston's basic design increase the number of variations (now using laser technology) that are machine-engraved on to new master plates. These are taken into the section of the building that looks most like a prison, for the chrome-covered nickel plates that go on to the printing machines are made behind bars.

There is a separate activity which is almost as important as making notes, and that is testing them to destruction. This takes on an experimental form in a squat building set apart from the others in which the Bank's scientists devise a variety of ingenious machines that compete to see which is most efficient at annihilation. Notes are boiled in Surf and Persil. There is a machine that rubs them away, another that crumples them up small or pricks them with pin holes until they fall apart. Other machines flex them and fold them until they can no longer stand the strain. Cost-saving theories are put to the test, like making paper out of old notes, or of plastic (neither beats cotton so far). The chief cashier asked for an ink that was guaranteed to last for 250 years and the scientists told him they were not able to test their results empirically, for the rheological properties of the ink are unlike Parker washable blue. (Rheology is a word with genuine utility in ink manufacture since it is the science dealing with the flow of matter.) Ink manufacture is actually a part of the design and development division and it is there that the ink oozes like a waterfall in slow motion from mangles that mix the pigment with the right resins and varnish and the proper amount of petroleum, and in the vat this ink is so thick it could be spread with a knife.

Destruction takes place on a much larger scale in the paid-note office, which once meant the office in the Bank that paid the bearer the sum of so many pounds, and is now where old notes go to disappear. Destroying notes is part of the cost of making them, and here the security involved is no less intense. Visitors are asked to leave all the bank notes in their possession in a locked box at the entrance. Since they enter without a note on their person, if they have any when they leave those notes must be stolen. Temptation is quickly diminished, however, by the sight of so much money. Packed in bundles and crated, £100 million begins to look more like waste paper than a lot of money.

There is a sound practical reason for destroying notes. As Wheatley observes: 'The best way to facilitate forgery is to have dirty bank notes.' Prodded by the chief cashier, who had in turn been bullied by the Treasury, strict limits have been imposed on the printing works' budget, and money is saved at Debden simply by keeping notes circulating in the system longer than the management would like. (Longer life means fewer notes produced, and thus savings on paper, ink and man hours.) Old notes that are returned to the printing works are sorted on machines, and millions are reissued: any note that will survive in an automatic telling machine is fit to be recycled. Of course, the clearing banks, complaining on behalf of their customers, want more new notes, and although the Bank is sympathetic and tries to pump a few more million new notes out, the best it can do is shift the blame to the Treasury, where it belongs.

Debden is where notes from London and the south are sorted, the job being done elsewhere by the Bank's regional branches. Since old notes are scrutinized more carefully than ever before, forgeries are turning up more regularly than they used to. Currently checkers are finding them at a rate of three forgeries per million five-pound notes and at a rate of twenty twenties per million. Since 522 million fivers were issued in 1986 this gives a rough tally of 1,566 forgeries, and, among 122 million twenties, 2,440 forgeries. This is not a great deal of money compared to the £12.3 billion of notes in circulation, but that forgers should succeed in passing any notes at all is a source of annoyance to the Bank. There are specimens of forged notes in a folder in the checking room in the paid-note office. They are poor things mostly, but the higher the denomination the more professional they look, and there was one fifty-pound note of which the forger could feel proud.

After the Second World War forged fivers, on the white paper used until 1957, turned up regularly; and no one ever discovered how much money made by the most successful forger of the British currency – the wartime German government – went into circulation. The Bank's experts maintain they have detected every forgery that has been presented to them; Wheatley himself exposed one in Leeds. The Germans were able to reproduce the Bank's paper; now forgers make use of the latest colour printing techniques, which were not available to their predecessors. Turning paper into money is an irresistible temptation, like an alchemist turning base metal into gold, and the determination to control forgery explains why even the notes that are so soiled that they are sent to London from the branches are checked randomly in Debden before being transported by conveyor, untouched by human hand, into automatically controlled incinerators which burn thirty-five million notes each week until the ash is completely unrecognizable as banknote waste. The furnaces and the chimney through which no ash can possibly escape were built at Debden in 1961 because the alternative at that time, the Battersea Power Station, might have allowed imperfectly burned notes to escape through the chimney – and the Bank has to replace notes which have been mutilated by fire. (Or, indeed, by other agents like washing machines: there is a small department at Debden which pieces together notes to verify claims for replacement.)

Doors on the blazing furnaces are closed by lock and chain, not to protect unwary visitors from an accident, but to protect the notes from the visitors. These notes give off a good heat, and the Bank, in something close to a parody of its passion for self-sufficiency, uses the energy generated by its burning millions to cut its fuel bill by a quarter, by heating part of the paid-note building. Money is the most economical available fuel.

The passion for security at Debden is intended to contribute to the sense of impregnability that is, as we have seen, part of the mystique of the Bank. But it is not mere propaganda, for the mystique lasts only as long as the money is safe. The Great Train Robbery in 1964 did the mystique no good and is taken most seriously at the Bank. The robbers took £3.5 million in English notes that were being brought from Glasgow by the clearing banks for recirculation in England. But as far as the eventual cost of the robbery went, that was only the beginning. 'The Train Robbery had a tremendous effect,' George Blunden told me in 1978. 'Before the Robbery, well over half the notes used by the public were drawn by the clearing banks from the Bank in London. After the Robbery we had to decentralize the operation further, because the banks wanted to withdraw money from our branches. But decentralization meant we had to rebuild our branches in Manchester, Leeds, Newcastle and Birmingham with larger security vaults; and enlarge the facilities in Southampton, Bristol and Liverpool. We've built a completely new note centre in Glasgow so that the Scots do not have to travel as far south as Newcastle to get their notes.' (Since then the Southampton and Liverpool branches have been closed and the note centre in Glasgow sold to the Scottish banks, which now have to go to Newcastle once more to obtain English notes.)

Now the plain blue trucks parked at the loading bay outside the printing works have armed guards and police cars to accompany them into Threadneedle Street or to the sidings where they are loaded on to container trains. (The Bank has never taken advantage of the fact that the printing works and Threadneedle Street are both on the Central Line.)

The printing works' broad production schedule is planned as much as five years in advance by the banking department, after it has studied estimates of demand for money produced on a model specially constructed by the economic department. The outline of this plan is necessarily broad, and it is refined each year, when more accurate assessments of the demand for various denominations are passed down the line to Debden. These forecasts would be expected to show, for instance, the steep rise in demand for ten-pound notes (up from 230 million in 1983 to 451 million in 1985), the increasing popularity of twenties (up from 86 million in 1985 to 122 million in 1986), and the fairly steady demand for fifties, which started at nine million in 1983 and had reached only 17 million by 1986. Firm orders are placed by the banking department every six months, for after that demand is predictable. It rises in the weeks before Christmas and in the days before a major national holiday; and within the week demand for money is slack on a Monday and high on a Friday.

The notes, having been cut, bundled and packed in wire cages with sealed locks, are stored in Debden, waiting to be issued. The exchange that turns these cages of expensively printed paper (notes were once produced at exactly three a penny, but the cost has risen to £10 per thousand notes, or one penny each) into real money takes place when the clearing banks make their own estimate of how much cash they will need, and go to the Bank of England to buy it. This transaction is often complicated by terms like 'fiduciary issue', but in practice it is perfectly straightforward. When the Midland Bank, for example, decides that it needs £100 million in banknotes, the man whose signature will be recognized at the Bank writes a cheque drawn on the Midland Bank for the sum of £100 million, which is handed to the driver of the armoured truck whose job is to collect it. He drives into the Bank from Lothbury and enters the covered courtyard called Bullion Yard, where he presents the Midland's cheque to the man from the issue department, and loads up cages of notes worth £100 million. Then he drives off and the cash is distributed to the branch network.

It is a convenience that seems all the more admirable because it does not cost us consumers anything. But someone pays, since the Bank, on behalf of the government, uses the Midland's £100 million cheque to pull off a trick so clever that hardly anyone knows how it is done.

As soon as it is presented, the issue department cashes the cheque, debiting the Midland's account at the Bank, and uses the money to buy securities worth £100 million from the banking department. These securities are a mixture of long-term government stock, short-term Treasury bills, some commercial bills and even company shares if they are as safe as, say, British Petroleum. Naturally, when the Midland returns the £100 million of notes after they have become irrevocably spoiled its account is credited again with £100 million; but while the notes are in use the Bank is collecting interest on the securities that the issue department has purchased from the banking department. This is a matter of earning money without spending any, and the Bank has a monopoly of this excellent business, since the Midland cannot go for its £100 million to another company whose price is competitive. In return for this monopoly, the Bank, having deducted the costs, hands over the profits to the government, which awarded it the monopoly under clause 6 of the Currency and Bank Notes Act, 1928. This Act transferred the power to issue all English notes from the Treasury to the Bank. (The first low-denomination notes in Britain this century were issued by the Treasury during the First World War to compensate for the shortage of gold coin. In the United States, the Treasury has always taken responsibility for the note issue, but Montagu Norman argued, as he would, that the prestige of the British currency would be greater if it bore the name of the Bank rather than the Treasury.) Consequently, the interest on the securities purchased by the issue department is paid daily by the Bank into the Treasury's account.

The end-of-the-year account is published in the Bank's annual report, and in the financial year that ended on 28 February 1987 the sum of the banknotes in circulation or held by the banking department amounted to £12,850,000,000. This was backed by securities at the Bank purchased by the issue department with the cash deposited by the clearing banks when they collected the notes, and the income earned in interest from these securities came to £1,411,341,000.

Deduct from that sum the cost of producing the banknotes (£30,685,000); the cost of issue, custody and payment of the notes (£14,623,000); and other odd expenses (£3,162,000), and you have the amount payable to the Treasury. This comes to £1,362,871,000 which shows that there is no better way in the world of making money than having a monopoly in making money.

It is such a neat trick that the Bank makes little of it, as though it were embarrassed by the ease with which the profit is made. But its discretion does not end there. For an organization whose whole reason for being is money, the Bank often appears to be conspicuously shy of talking about it. Curiously enough, for a generation after the Second World War the Bank's policy-makers took hardly any notice of money. The first hint of a change was detectable in 1970, and that date makes a good starting-point for this story of the Bank of England's identity crisis.

3

Leslie O'Brien: Last of the Gentlemen

Leslie O'Brien was either the last Governor of the hermetic, conde-
scending Bank of England as it once was, or the first Governor of the
more open and vulnerable institution it has become. Perhaps he was
both. He joined the Bank while it still inhabited Soane's building, in
1926, aged nineteen, in circumstances that almost parody the institution. His father was a member of Roehampton Cricket Club and when
he mentioned his son's interest in economics a fellow member suggested
the Bank of England. O'Brien was approved by Lord Revelstoke, one
of the directors, and joined straight from Wandsworth Grammar
School. But that was common enough; very few recruits had degrees,
though most came from public school and a few had money of their
own. It was still a gentleman's occupation; indeed, O'Brien's passport
said 'gentleman of the Bank of England'. The atmosphere was
Dickensian, and many of the young recruits were fairly idle. Not
O'Brien.

Before the outbreak of war, O'Brien managed to extricate himself
from the routine of Threadneedle Street, working on a League of
Nations committee concerned with problem loans in the Balkans; and
the introduction of exchange control after the outbreak of war in 1939
provided him with his first real opportunity to display his talents for
organization and hard work. By 1943 he was private secretary to
Montagu Norman (his last), and he moved rapidly through the hierarchy, becoming chief cashier in 1955. His name appeared on banknotes
for seven years (including the very last crisp white five-pound note).
The post was the summit of his ambition.

He was coasting towards retirement as an executive director
when Lord Cromer was Governor in 1966, but Cromer incurred the
wrath of George Brown and was ousted at the end of his five-year
term. O'Brien became the first Governor in the history of the Bank to
have come up through the ranks of the staff, and, like many veterans
who make it to the top job, he thought the organization was healthy
enough. This was so of bank supervision, for instance. The Bank had
always taken its responsibility for supervision of the banks and the
money markets for granted, since one of the duties of the principal of
the discount office was to answer queries about credit-worthiness. He
was the man who collected intelligence in the City, combining it with
the agreeable social function of lunching and dining with the banking
community. It was considered axiomatic that the banks themselves
operated proper financial control systems, and that whenever the Bank

required statistical information it only had to ask. The Bank advised prudence always, but never thought it necessary to impose strict limits on the relationship between loans on the books and capital reserves; guidelines were good enough. Being grown men, they accepted that the odd bounder would break the rules, but the club had ways of seeing that no one did so twice. James Keogh was the principal of the discount office while O'Brien was Governor and he ran a tight ship, with a staff of only fifteen. 'It was rudimentary, but that was largely because nothing more pervasive was necessary,' says O'Brien. After all, they were all in the same boat.

When Barclays Bank proposed merging with Lloyds and Martins Banks, the Governor disapproved of the idea. He said so, and the idea was dropped. 'They were nice sort of fellows who played by the rules,' O'Brien recalls. He interpreted the rules and sometimes administered them, gently and privately, like the chairman of the general committee of a club. Then, as now, the Bank emphasized the importance of sound management of City banks, and O'Brien recalls the case of one recalcitrant banker who had run a small merchant bank for years. By his eightieth birthday the discount office began to drop hints. Had he, they asked nicely, given any thought to appointing a successor? Since he was impervious to such suggestions, the problem was passed upwards to the Governor. Not wishing to appear too formal, O'Brien asked him to lunch, at which he said firmly that the Bank believed that the time had come for the banker to go. 'He took it rather hard,' says O'Brien. 'Within two days he was dead.'

Leslie O'Brien's manner was mild and loyal, but there was one area in which he thought the Bank could do better. This was economic policy, where the Bank had played a passive role as executor rather than originator, partly because the old public-school crowd was not strong on policy. To equip the Bank, O'Brien promoted economists and encouraged them to hire more people like them from the universities. John Fforde, who had worked in Whitehall and taught at Nuffield before joining the Bank, became chief cashier. Kit McMahon was moving through the hierarchy at speed, and a young economist named Charles Goodhart was writing papers that emphasized the importance of money. The last word on money had been written in 1959 in the Radcliffe Report, which had concluded that the unpredictable velocity of changes in the supply of money in the economy was incidental to the thing that counted most: broad liquidity and interest-rate policy. This had remained the orthodox view.

Goodhart questioned this, insisting on the importance of the money supply, and the monetary theme proved useful to senior men in the Bank who wanted to change the rules used by the banking system to control credit. And when changes were introduced in September 1971 it was the Governor, not the Chancellor, who made the announcement, in a paper entitled *Competition and Credit Control*, which was largely the work of the chief cashier, John Fforde.

Since the war the British high-street banks, the clearing banks, had operated a cartel on the instructions of the government. So that the Treasury could control the amount of money loaned by banks, this amount was rationed, and the rates of interest on loans were the same wherever the money came from. This stern system of credit control sapped the energy and enthusiasm of the banks, and O'Brien noticed that they had become adept at refusing business. Customers were growing restive, and other financial institutions that were not operating under the auspices of the discount office, like hire-purchase companies and overseas banks, and credit institutions unrecognized by the discount office, known as secondary banks, were edging into the money market.

The solution proposed by *Competition and Credit Control* was to allow a free market to operate: 'to permit the price mechanism to function efficiently in the allocation of credit and to free the banks from rigidities and restraints that have for a long time inhibited them', was how O'Brien described the changes at the time. The new regulations imposed indirect controls. The Bank could still call for special deposits from the clearers to curb lending, but the main instrument for controlling the volume of credit was to be the interest rate, which now became known as minimum lending rate or M L R, instead of bank rate.

Competition and Credit Control was the first evidence that the Bank proposed playing an active role in economic policy. A joint committee of the Bank and the Treasury had met under the chairmanship of Sir Douglas Allen, the Treasury's permanent secretary, to discuss a monetary policy and changes in the system of credit rationing, but *Competition and Credit Control* appeared before the joint committee had reported, and emphasis on monetary control, by means of changes in the interest rate, was an instance of the Bank reasserting its traditional role as controller of money in the economy. Allen was annoyed at the Bank's unilateralism, but did not make an issue of it. Personal relations between the Bank and the Treasury were unusually good at the time. He had known O'Brien for years, having first met him in the company of his own distinguished predecessor, Sir William Armstrong. But O'Brien's friendships were not confined to civil servants. He had remarkably good relations with James Callaghan and Roy Jenkins (whom he considered the finest Chancellor since the war). His rapport with Anthony Barber, Heath's Chancellor after the death of Iain Macleod, was not so close, but its condition was not so fragile that a civil servant like Allen could inhibit it. Allen comforted himself with the knowledge that the Bank's policy in *Competition and Credit Control* could never really work as an act of independence. To function properly, the policy depended on the discipline of the interest rate, and that was applied by the Treasury and not the Bank.

O'Brien's first term ended in 1971, and Barber had wondered whether he ought to reappoint him for another five years. The Governor was shocked to hear about the Chancellor's doubts. Since he was the first Governor to be appointed from the ranks, O'Brien felt the Bank might be humiliated if he were asked to serve only one term; so he did a deal with Barber – if the government reappointed him, he would not serve a full five-year term. O'Brien expected to resign after two years, in 1973, and he was as good as his word. It was funny, but by the time he was ready to go, the Chancellor wanted him to stay. The consequences of *Competition and Credit Control* were becoming an embarrassment to the Treasury, and the chief perpetrator of that policy was about to retire just when they would have liked someone with whom to share the blame.

It had gone wrong from the beginning. The Bank's purpose was admirable, for it had wished to ease the restrictions on credit so that British industry no longer experienced any difficulty in obtaining the capital it needed for expansion. Unfortunately, by the time the controls were relaxed at the end of 1971 British industry was not expanding, and there was no demand on the banks for new industrial capital. The demand came instead from the property market, which was growing so fast that it attracted investors, many of whom did not grasp that they could lose money by speculating in property. Prudence had gone out of fashion, and one reason for this was the growth of the secondary banks. Although they had never been defined as banks by the Bank, they were lending money to virtually any property dealer who poked his head through their doors. The clearing banks had plenty to lend themselves, and since industry made no demands for it, they were happy to lend to secondary banks. Traditionally, the latter had been small deposit-taking institutions specializing in consumer credit and personal loans, often secured by second mortgages. Now they became big business, lending to developers who were willing to pay more for their money than the clearers would have charged. But the clearers would probably not have lent them money at all; these clients were splendid financiers, and imprudent borrowers.

These trends began to show up in the statistics in the summer of 1972. The money supply began to rise dangerously, and it was time to exercise the discipline that had been outlined in *Competition and Credit Control* in such circumstances – interest rates ought to be put up sharply. The Bank said so; it pleaded with the Treasury to agree to raise interest rates, but the Chancellor said no. The reason was that Anthony Barber was not free to do so. The Prime Minister, Edward Heath, was more concerned about rising unemployment. He wanted to make a last attempt to break through to a higher rate of economic growth by encouraging investment, and since higher interest rates would have precisely the opposite effect Heath declared that they were out of the question – at least until there was no longer any choice.

The government's options narrowed in July 1973 when minimum lending rate went up to $11\frac{1}{2}$ per cent. This was to prevent a run on sterling after the currency was allowed to float. It was a momentous year in the history of international finance and marked the final crack-up of the Bretton Woods system, which had kept international currencies remarkably stable since 1944, but the implications were lost on the British secondary banking system, which did not think it was their problem and went on lending money recklessly. In the summer the Bank tried to curb the flood by using one of its reserve weapons and calling for special deposits from the clearing banks to reduce the volume of money available for lending. In mid-November the government finally recognized the inevitability of a régime of high interest rates and let MLR rise to 13 per cent – a level unprecedented in recent economic experience. But the Bank and the government were both too late. That same month a secondary bank called London and County Securities was unable to roll over, or renew, loans it had made in the money market. A study of its balance-sheet showed that it had a terminal liquidity problem – because its loans were greater than its deposits, the bank had borrowed more than it could repay. This was the beginning of the secondary banking crisis and the awful implications of it were spelled out (more than four years later) by Gordon Richardson, who had been Governor for a mere four months when the crisis broke.

> In the last days of 1973, in November or December, we found ourselves confronted with the collapse of several deposit-taking institutions and with the clear and present danger at that time of a rapidly escalating crisis of confidence, which threatened other deposit-taking institutions and which, if left unchecked, would have quickly passed into the banking system proper. In those circumstances I had no hesitation about what the Bank's action should be. It was to stop a potential avalanche before its full potential could be developed . . .

A document prepared for the Wilson Inquiry into the City spelled out the threat to the big banks:

> While the U K clearing banks still appeared secure from the domestic effects of any run, their international exposure was such that the risk to external confidence was a matter of concern for themselves as well as the Bank. The problem was to avoid a widening circle of collapse through the contagion of fear.

This was the Bank of England acting as lender of last resort – the classic role of a central bank – and playing its part in getting through 'the worst moment for the British economy since the war' (Douglas Allen). Because the banking crisis was accompanied by the three-day week, the miners' strike and the fall of Edward Heath, one embarrassing question was largely overlooked: why had the Bank as supervisor of the banking system allowed the crisis to develop at all?

The answer lay in the discount office. The reason why Leslie O'Brien's position in the history of the Bank – as the last of the old Governors or the first of the new – is uncertain is that while his competition policy was characteristic of the new, open Bank, the system of bank supervision belonged squarely to the tradition of the old, clubbable Bank. There is a provocative snapshot of the system in the early 1970s which was produced many years later in the report of the tribunal into the operations of the Crown Agents from 1967 to 1974.

The Crown Agents became infected by the same exaggerated notions of finance as the secondary banks, lending money to financiers like William Stern, the property developer who became Britain's then largest-ever bankrupt. Eventually, the government bailed out the Crown Agents, one consequence being a tribunal that laid bare the operating methods of Whitehall and the Bank. No one emerged with credit from the tribunal's final report: John Page, who had succeeded John Fforde as chief cashier, was accused of 'a lapse from accepted standards', and John Fforde, now executive director, was 'criticized'. This judgement caused anger and distress in the Bank, especially as the tribunal appeared to accept its basic defence – that since the Crown Agents were an organization in the public sector, responsibility for supervising them lay with the Treasury and the Ministry of Overseas Development.

But the Bank had had long and tiresome experience of the Crown Agents. They had bought an unsuitable merchant bank, evaded exchange-control regulations, taken advantage of a privileged position in the Treasury bill market, and had actually had the audacity to overdraw on their account at the Bank. In 1971 O'Brien told the Treasury of the Bank's dissatisfaction with the management of the Crown Agents, but this concern was not elaborated on during a subsequent inquiry. An investigation begun by James Keogh in the discount office was not followed up, and nothing came of the proposal to subject the Crown Agents to the credit-control system used by the discount office to monitor banks.

The tribunal report (published in 1982 after most of its subjects had retired) relentlessly exposed the way in which information was allowed to slip through the gaps in the Bank's organizational structure. This was the indictment:

> The risk of important points being overlooked or of advice not being properly considered was intensified by the Bank's methods of working. Much of its work was done orally and informally. The Governor had daily meetings with the deputy governor, the executive directors and the chief cashier. The chief cashier had weekly meetings with the heads of other departments and with the principal of the discount office. We are told that the Crown Agents were sometimes discussed at these meetings. In addition, there were occasional discussions specifically about the Crown Agents. But the decisions taken in these discussions and the views formulated were either not

recorded at all, or were recorded only in a brief manuscript note scribbled on the top of a minute and often not copied to all concerned. As a result, when junior staff who had not been involved in earlier discussions were sent – sometimes at very short notice – to represent the Bank at interdepartmental meetings, they were not familiar with the background or the Bank's views, and there was no file to which they could turn for a record of the Bank's previous involvement and thinking. Government departments looking for advice from those representing the Bank at such meetings had little idea of how inadequately informed they often were.

This oral tradition was one reason why the Bank was not always clearly heard in Whitehall, where it is unfailing practice to record conversations in memoranda and minutes. Douglas Allen remarks that he would never have considered a conversation, even with the Governor, about an issue like the Crown Agents as a formal warning of trouble. He expected everything in writing. The tribunal concluded that the Bank's arcane working methods were a factor in this dismal affair: 'The test of such a method is whether it works. In this case it did not.'

Its concentration on the Bank's style of management gave the tribunal's conclusion a wider application than merely to the Crown Agents. That this case was merely a symptom of a general malaise became clear during the secondary banking crisis. O'Brien recalls another disquieting lesson: 'We did think that, through the discount office, we had sufficient insight to realize that banks would not go over the top. With hindsight we could see that was not the case.' The truth was that the Bank of England could trust neither the banks themselves nor its own discount office to detect imprudent behaviour.

Central banking in a crisis is like a conjuring trick that creates the illusion that nothing is happening. What is actually happening, but is cleverly concealed, is the contagious spread of fear. The Lifeboat operation launched by the Bank to contain the secondary banking crisis was a classic central-banking operation, and in order to understand why, it is useful to outline the way in which a catastrophe develops.

Stage one is the liquidity problem in the fringe or secondary banks. Depositors, worried about the safety of their cash, withdraw it, beginning a run on the bank. The money that has been withdrawn often finds its way into the clearing banks, which do not pay as much interest but which are more secure.

Stage two begins when the fringe bank is unable to meet its obligations in the money market. Because it has become suspect, other banks are unwilling to continue to lend or roll over their loans, and the fringe bank does not have enough depositors' money on its books to redeem debts when they fall due.

In stage three the credit-worthiness of the clearing banks is weakened because of the loans they have made to fringe banks. The clearers borrow in international money markets, and once it seems possible that they will incur substantial losses in their dealings with the fringe banks, international banks begin to refuse to roll over loans to the clearers. Confidence in the big banks wavers. If one is identified as particularly vulnerable, a run begins.

In stage four fear spreads to the currency markets, causing heavy foreign-exchange losses; and any financial institution whose loan book is heavily dependent on a weak sector of the economy – such as property – is now in danger of collapse. This is the brink of a financial Armageddon. That is stage five, when the whole international banking system breaks down.

The Lifeboat operation to prevent this awesome happening was formally launched on 28 December 1973, when the English and Scottish clearing banks met under the chairmanship of the deputy governor, Sir Jasper Hollom. Once they had identified the twenty-one fringe banks that were in danger and capable of salvage, their first objective was to plough funds that had been withdrawn by worried depositors back into the reserves of these fringe banks. This was re-cycling money: having been withdrawn from fringe banks and deposited with the clearer, the same funds were used by the clearers to bolster the fringe banks. By March 1974 £400 million had been advanced by members of the Lifeboat – with the Bank itself contributing 10 per cent to demonstrate its commitment. Recycling was something the clearers understood. But £400 million was not enough.

In the spring of 1974 the great inflation began. Oil prices had quadrupled the previous November and at home wage increases went out of control after the settlement of the miners' strike. Next the property boom collapsed (this was when the Stern Group went bankrupt). The assets of fringe banks were squeezed by the combination of inflation and falling property values, and a second run on the fringe banks began. It was stopped only when the Lifeboat banks *guaranteed* the deposits in the fringe banks. They had to do this to preserve confidence in the Lifeboat itself – to keep it afloat.

Conditions grew rougher in the summer of 1974, when Bankhaus Herstatt in Frankfurt and the Franklin National Bank in New York collapsed. In London, the distress caused by the falling property prices spread to large finance houses like the First National Finance Corporation and United Dominions Trust, which had substantial property portfolios. The cost of propping up these institutions raised the money committed to the Lifeboat to £1,200 million by the end of 1974 – which amounted to 40 per cent of the capital and reserves of the banks involved. This was too much for the clearers, especially as they thought money was being provided to bolster banks that were basically bust, and they jumped ship.

The Bank of England, however, felt it was too soon to quit, explaining why after the event to the Wilson Committee:

> In all these circumstances, domestic and international, the Bank felt impelled to shoulder the additional risk implied by the unwillingness of the other members of the Lifeboat to extend their commitments beyond £1,200 million. That the Bank's concern was not financial was subsequently underlined when the National Westminster Bank found it necessary at the beginning of December 1974 to issue a statement to the effect that current rumours that they were receiving support from the Bank were without foundation.

And that was not the end of it. The maximum overall total of support committed to the Lifeboat reached £1,285 million in March 1975. Only then did the sums involved begin to fall. Later that year, however, the Bank supported operations outside the Lifeboat, one of which proved to be the most controversial of its actions during this crisis. One of the companies it chose to save was Slater Walker Limited, the justification being the 300,000 investors in the Group's unit trust and the £75 million loans outstanding to foreign banks.

For the Bank it was a matter of confidence in the London foreign-exchange market. To the critics of the Bank, who now included the clearers, it was an astonishing error of judgement, for James Slater's career had been nurtured inside the bubble and when it burst he was certain to be one of its victims. Although he retired from his bank with discredit, Slater Walker itself was allowed to survive, and it became a monument to the Bank's extreme nervousness at the prospect of the collapse of any bank in the City of London. It even moved in to save a secondary bank called Edward Bates for the same reason: its debts in the Eurocurrency markets threatened the City's international reputation. This was a grave embarrassment for the Bank, since Edward Bates had been licensed to deal in foreign currency in December 1973, when the warning bells were already deafening.

But Gordon Richardson was unrepentant. He did not seek to explain the Bank's actions until 1978, when he gave his bloodcurdling account of the crisis to the Commons Select Committee on Nationalized Industries.

> I have seen criticism that some of the institutions did not, to put it mildly, match the highest standards. We had to support some institutions which did not themselves deserve support on their merits, and, indeed, institutions which fell outside the Bank's established range of supervisory responsibilities. But I felt, as I saw the tide coming in, that it was necessary to take the Bank beyond the banking system proper, for which it was responsible, into those deposit-taking institutions, because collapse there was capable of letting the wave come on to the institutions themselves; and the fact that very rapidly we had to extend our support to a wider circle, which included some reputable banking institutions, showed that our instinct that we were on very treacherous ground was sound . . . there are no doubt things one would have done differently with the benefit of hindsight; but I have absolutely no hesitation in saying that, faced with the same circumstances again – regrettable though they were – I would take the same strategic decision and would act in the same way.

Richardson's assured defence of the Bank was an indication of how the restoration of confidence in the banking system had buttressed the confidence of the Bank itself. Captaincy of the Lifeboat was one of those glorious episodes in the history of the Bank that became part of its mystique. But the crisis had revealed deficiencies as well.

The bank found a scapegoat. The principal of the discount office, James Keogh, took early retirement and went to work for the Singapore Monetary Authority, but anyone who understood the meaning of a nod and a wink got the message from the Bank that old Keogh was to blame: the trouble, old boy, was that he kept everything in his head, said the men who stayed behind him. Since there was no mechanism for bank supervision, there was nowhere else for Keogh to keep it but his head. There were few people with whom to share the information he received, and he soon got the impression that those who were in a position to listen to him were not much interested in what he said. The truth was that the secondary banking crisis revealed an institutional failure, not a personnel problem. The Bank had taken its role as supervisor for granted but had not taken it seriously. Its distaste for legislation of any kind being allowed to intrude on its private relationship with the City meant that there was not even a satisfactory statutory definition of a bank. A bank was what the Governor of the Bank of England considered a bank.

George Blunden was put in charge of a new division of banking supervision, but it was clear in 1974 that more than a change in personnel was required and that one outcome of the episode would be a new law to regulate banks. The content of the Bill would emerge from consultations between the City and the Bank, and the Bank and the Treasury. How those turned out would be influenced by the relationship between the Governor and the Chancellor.

In later years, when the secondary banking crisis was being mulled over, with the benefit of the Governor's hindsight, it was easy to overlook the fact that Richardson kept in the background while the Bank's public position in the first hectic months was taken by Sir Jasper Hollom, who remained in day-to-day charge of the Lifeboat. While he worked himself in, Gordon Richardson had kept a deliberately low personal profile, and when colleagues asked cocky young clearing bankers, whose rounds took them to the Bank, where they had been, they would reply: 'To see the Tomb of the Unknown Governor.'

4

Gordon Richardson: Elegant Meritocrat

When Gordon Richardson was at Nottingham High School he was a stylish batsman, a rugby player, and clever enough to win a place at Caius College, Cambridge. But the best indication of what he might become when he grew up is that he was head boy, thus displaying that combination of responsibility, authority and ambition which impresses adults. Head boys do not give older people trouble.

Richardson has never shown any interest in autobiography, and has revealed little more about his childhood than is necessary to satisfy *Who's Who*: born in Nottingham on 25 November 1915, elder son of John Robert and Nellie Richardson. His father worked for a food wholesaler's in Nottingham; his mother was thought to be proud, strong-minded and independent. The family was apparently not well off, but comfortable (his father owned a car, a true status symbol among the boys at Nottingham High School in the 1930s).

At Cambridge he studied law, though he had not time to practise before the outbreak of war. He had been an officer in the Territorials, and in 1939 became commanding officer of the South Notts Hussars Yeomanry for eighteen months, before finding a more suitable niche in the army – as a staff officer, eventually acting as a link between the chiefs of staff and the headquarters of the army in north-west Europe. He won the MBE in 1944 while still in his twenties. In 1941 he had married Margaret, daughter of a famous preacher, Canon Dick Sheppard of St Martin-in-the-Fields in central London, where Richardson intended to live. King's Road was more to his taste than the provinces, and the couple bought a house in Chelsea Square.

Called to the Bar in 1946, Richardson specialized in company law. He was diligent, intelligent, with a good courtroom manner, and would no doubt have gone far had he not quit the Bar at the age of forty. When good barristers reach that age the Lord Chancellor's office is already thinking about their futures, deciding whether they should become distinguished judges or flashy QCs; either way, they are committed to the law for the rest of their lives. (Unless they become politicians, an option Richardson seems not to have considered.) The predictability of life in the law is a forbidding prospect for many clever men on the brink of middle age, and when Richardson decided to make the break in 1955 it was a bit of a gamble, but not much of a risk. The odds must have been better than even that something would turn up in the City or in industry; and his first job at the Industrial and Commercial Finance Corporation blended the two. But this was only a prelude to the sort of job he really wanted. His friends suggested he should go to a small clearing bank like Williams and Glyns, but he chose the merchant bankers J. Henry Schroder Wagg when he was offered a directorship. (In those days men who wanted to become Governor did not work for clearing banks.) He had made the acquaintance of the chairman when he was asked for legal advice on the merger between Schroder and Wagg, and when he began work in the City in 1957 he soon made up for lost time. Within a couple of years he was managing director. He was made deputy chairman in 1960, and chairman in 1962. Running a bank suited him; his real interest lay in getting things done, also known as exercising power.

He appeared reserved, seeking influence rather than celebrity, but his circle of friends grew wider during his forays into public service. Chairing the committee established by the Chancellor to consider whether value added tax ought to be adopted, he made the acquaintance of Sir Henry Benson, the accountant from Coopers and Lybrand who was a great figure in the City. (His friendship proved more influential than Richardson's report; it came out against VAT.) His circle spread further when he sat on the Jenkins Committee on Company Law, and when he accepted the vice-chairmanship of Lloyds Bank.

Richardson was a member of Brooks's Club, but not the sort of man to take pot luck with fellow members at the bar. He preferred the company of like-minded men, whom he invited back to Chelsea Square or whom he met at dining clubs – The Club and The Parlour were two – where men of affairs from politics, industry and the City would talk shop. They were the elegant end of the meritocracy, and one colleague who joined him at the Bank remarks: 'He had a merchant prince's idea of the role of City grandees, and felt they knew as well as anyone how to run the country.' The identity of those he regarded as City grandees was revealed shortly after he became Governor, when he asked them to chair working groups to study the City: they were men like Eric Faulkner, chairman of Lloyds Bank, Sir Henry Fisher, a High Court judge whom he had recruited at Schroders, and Ian Fraser, a former director-general of the takeover panel.

At Schroders he developed the corporate finance department. He might have come from the Bar, but he was commercially adept at poaching industrial customers from other merchant banks. His ambition was to transform Schroders into a great international investment bank, partly because he found Wall Street more open and more profitable. He spent a good deal of time there, building the business and the reputation of Schroders, before his grand plan foundered on xenophobic banking regulations. A colleague from those days recalls: 'This encouraged his instinctive feeling that financial services should be as flexible and non-statutory as possible.' But that was a rare defeat. By the late 1960s Richardson's position in the City was secure.

During the years at Schroders it was already possible to identify some of the attributes of Richardson's style of management. First, he mistrusted complex organizational structures ('get the people right' was an essential component of the theory), and he was anxious to allow the right people time to develop their arguments. He was oddly reluctant to take decisions, preferring to establish a consensus, even if it did take an unconscionable time to do so.

A colleague at Schroders commented on one further attribute of Richardson in the 1960s: 'He was absolutely fascinated by the style and mystique of the Bank, and he always knew who to go and see – Balfour in the overseas department, Cooke in the discount office.' He was a natural candidate for the Court and was finally appointed a member on 13 January 1967, when the *Financial Times* wrote: 'There will be widespread approval and pleasure in the City today on the appointment of Mr Gordon Richardson to the Court of the Bank of England. Few men inside or outside of merchant banking have risen to City stardom more quickly and deservedly.' It had taken him exactly a decade. Richardson attended his first meeting of the Court on 17 March and was immediately plunged into the ritual of the Bank. As the newest member, he was delighted to act out the traditional charade of notifying the Bank official waiting at the door of the Court's decision regarding bank rate (a decision the Court had not taken, and that the official already knew).

Had Leslie O'Brien not been reappointed when his first term ended in 1971, two Whitehall permanent secretaries had a chance of becoming Governor: Sir William Armstrong, who had run the Treasury, and Sir Eric Roll, who had run the Department of Economic Affairs until 1968. But by 1973 Armstrong, as indispensable head of the Cabinet Office, was regarded as Edward Heath's 'deputy Prime Minister', and Roll had joined S. G. Warburg and fallen out of the running. There being no strong internal contender at the Bank, Gordon Richardson became the natural candidate. He had an established position, an international reputation, and a bonus was that he really wanted to be Governor. He was the City's head boy, though this was not the analogy that occurred to him. I met him some years after he took the job and asked whether the position of Governor inspired fear in others. 'I would not have thought the office of Governor still commands fear,' he replied, 'though I do think it commands a certain degree of respect and goodwill. It's true of Prime Ministers and Popes too, isn't it?'

The practical aspect of this splendid Governorship was soon observed in Whitehall. The weekly meetings at the Treasury began by Montagu Norman had become a fixed point in a Governor's diary. Some established a comfortable relationship with the permanent secretary, who, as his title implies, is a more enduring figure than the Chancellor: O'Brien had close contacts with William Armstrong and with his successor, Douglas Allen, who was the permanent secretary when Richardson became Governor on 1 July 1973 (he was only the fifth in fifty years). Within a few months Allen noted that Richardson had no intention of following O'Brien's practice. When Richardson arrived at the Treasury in the Governor's Rolls-Royce he was shown to the Chancellor's room. If comparisons were to be drawn to indicate his position in the hierarchy of government, he wanted people to assume that he was a man of Cabinet rank. His relationship with Douglas Allen remained most civil (indeed, on Allen's retirement Richardson snapped him up as an advisor); but when Douglas Wass succeeded Allen, relations between the Governor and the permanent secretary were, says one Treasury man, 'very up and down, mostly down' – despite the fact that Wass was another old boy of Nottingham High School.

In the Bank itself Richardson's attitudes often surprised senior officials who came into contact with him. For instance, he was acutely conscious of what newspapers wrote about the Bank, much more so than O'Brien, who had an old Bank man's disregard for the press. First editions would arrive at Richardson's home in Mayfair (he had moved up a peg) before midnight and if an item displeased him, a press officer was instructed to see if something could not be done about it. He worried about adverse comment at Books (see p. 28) the following morning, which was thought to show unnecessary sensitivity; perhaps even a lack of confidence.

As for writing his speeches, this process soon became legendary in the Bank. Richardson would sit behind his desk with a row of people from various grades who would discuss the speech as though it were the subject of a seminar. Drafts were prepared, taken apart, and put together again very slowly. The leading participants in these sessions were the Bank's economists, for the chief cashier, John Page, found he had neither the time nor the patience for them. The economists dominated the policy-making process at the Bank in the mid-1970s: Kit McMahon, then director of the overseas department; John Fforde, director of home finance; Christopher Dow, the head of the economics department; and Charles Goodhart, the specialist adviser on monetary economics. They proved a particularly distinguished group of teachers, for, as one of them recalls: 'To begin with, Gordon Richardson didn't have any idea about economic policy. It took him two years to settle into the saddle.' Yet it was economic policy that mattered most to him, for he considered the Bank's most important single role was to make an independent contribution to policy, especially in monetary affairs and exchange-rate policy. So he applied his mind to it, much as a judge would do.

Almost six months passed before Richardson made his first major speech as Governor, and it was a corker. The headline over the lead story in *The Times* in January 1974 read 'Deficit threatens/austerity up/to 1984, says/Bank Governor'. Here was a central banker taking a long view of the economy and it was distinctly stormy. Richardson saw the problem as being huge balance-of-payments deficits, stretching into the 1980s. Oil prices were up enormously, of course, but the Governor did not blame them. The solution he outlined was to channel most of the increase in national output over a whole decade into correcting the deficit and financing North Sea oil. He proposed what most heads of central banks do when they see trouble ahead: people had a duty to tighten their belts, and accept lower standards of living. The effect of this speech was staggering. On the day the Governor spoke sterling fell to lower than ever before against the dollar ($2.1885). Later in the week the Bank had to support the pound, and at the weekend the *Sunday Express* had stern words for the Governor. 'We just cannot afford any more speeches from you, Mr Richardson,' read its headline. The Governor, having burned his fingers, kept his head down for a while after that.

He did not, however, have to worry about the reactions of Edward Heath and Anthony Barber, since they lost office in the General Election on 28 February 1974, and were never to regain it.

Denis Healey, whose experience of economic management was no greater than Richardson's, became Chancellor of the Exchequer, and Richardson concentrated on getting to know him well. Since they were both ambitious men absorbed by power, who liked listening to arguments develop, and who shared musical tastes, the relationship showed some promise.

Richardson also indulged in covert public-relations activities. He did not like answering journalists' questions in public and hardly ever spoke for the record, but he was willing to invite City and economics editors to dinner, where he could speak discreetly and entirely off the record. He also invited senior men from the Trades Union Congress – Jack Jones, Hugh Scanlon and Len Murray – not because he sympathized with their objectives, but because he understood that the country would not run without them. He had corporatist tastes in politics in the mid-1970s, but so did many others in public life.

His public appearances in 1975 were few and far between but there was no way of evading the Mansion House speech at the Lord Mayor's banquet in October, and, as a central banker ought, Richardson declared his anxiety about the effect of Labour's spending spree on the Public Sector Borrowing Requirement. The speech contained two other points which revealed what he was learning about economics in the long sessions with his advisers:

> There is much debate over the appropriate role of monetary policy in the present circumstance. For my part I do not doubt that it has an important and powerful influence on the economy – though the force and timing of its impact may be difficult to predict. I also believe that, in view of the overriding importance of moderating inflation – a problem to be seen in the context not just of this winter, but of the next two or three years – we should maintain a moderate pace of monetary expansion.
>
> I think it is now generally recognized that the reduction on the deficit will require not only the cautious planning of public expenditure for some years ahead, but also a mechanism of control over expenditure which is effective in the short run.

These were the motifs for the preoccupations of the Bank during 1976 and 1977. In the previous two years it had been absorbed with problems left on its doorstep by the secondary bankers and the clearers. The action, moving west to Whitehall, and then much further west to Washington DC, now had more to do with politics than banking.

In just half a decade, between 1971 and 1976, the world's economy had changed utterly. For a generation after the Bretton Woods conference in 1944, at which the United States government effectively took on the management of the international financial system, the world economy had been stable. Much of the world's post-war trade was transacted in dollars, and an attraction of the system was the agreement of the Americans to exchange these dollars earned by overseas nations for gold. The system worked wonderfully well as long as the American economy retained its natural vigour and strength. However, a number of factors conspired to sap it of that strength in the late 1960s. In 1966 President Lyndon Johnson, deciding that America was powerful enough to pursue a policy of both guns and butter, refused to increase taxes despite the growing costs of the war in Vietnam. Consequently, inflation began to germinate, and as it did so the competitiveness of the West German and Japanese economies, now thoroughly recovered from the war, eroded the American pre-eminence in export markets.

The certainties of the old system were first undermined in 1971, when the administration closed the gold window and dollars were no longer automatically convertible. Then the dollar was devalued, and by 1973 the currencies of the world's leading industrial nations no longer stood in fixed relationships to each other, but had begun to float. Once the disciplines of the Bretton Woods network disappeared, international economic policy became a free-for-all. The final attempt to restore order foundered in the autumn of 1973, and a few weeks later the swingeing increases in the price of oil doomed any lingering hope for a restoration of a Bretton Woods type of collaboration. Inflation had already set in across much of the world and throughout 1974 it grew progressively worse. Central bankers – custodians of the currency, after all – were the first public figures to be seriously alarmed.

The monthly meetings of the Bank for International Settlements in Basle provided the setting for central bankers to share their problems in private. Richardson became a regular visitor to Basle, and there he met a different kind of economist, people with as much if not more power than himself, who had trained as economists, like the Chairman of the Governors of the Federal Reserve, Arthur Burns, and Otmar

Emminger, the President of the Bundesbank. Without ever becoming followers, they took a professional interest in the work of the monetarist school, whose most vocal member was Milton Friedman. He won the Nobel Prize for economics in 1976, and the school was known as the Chicago School, after the university at which he taught. Since his theory was founded on a rejection of the work of John Maynard Keynes, Friedman was an audacious figure. He insisted that the orthodox economic establishment was leading the world to ruin by sticking to the management of demand as the basis of economic policy. Friedman's case was that governments ignored money at their peril, especially when the most severe threat to world stability was inflation and not unemployment. There was a doctrinaire quality about Friedman's work that did not appeal to central bankers like Burns and Emminger, but they could see some virtue in monetarism. The Federal Reserve had begun to establish targets for the growth of monetary aggregates in the American economy, and these were much discussed at Basle. The central bankers were interested in monetarism not as an economic doctrine, but as a different method of approaching economic problems. They even had a name for their version: 'practical monetarism'. They hoped it might be a way of getting politicians to take inflation seriously.

Indeed, by 1976 Richardson's interest in changing the way the British government thought about economics had become entirely practical. Overseas politicians as well as central bankers were losing confidence in the capacity of the Labour administration to manage the economy. Harold Wilson and Tony Benn were two of the reasons why, but the statistics also told a grim tale.

The government was already spending £12 billion more than it raised in taxes, inflation was 23.4 per cent and the balance of payments was deteriorating. The pound was valued at just over $2.00 throughout the winter of 1975–6 but it was due for a fall unless the government cut public spending. In the Treasury Sir Douglas Wass recommended that a virtue be made out of this. He proposed a devaluation of some 5 per cent – to $1.90 – to make British goods more competitive abroad and to reduce the balance-of-payments deficit. But the Treasury wanted to allow the value of the pound to fall without its being announced as policy. Devaluation was to be engineered covertly, by reducing interest rates, thus making sterling less attractive to the foreign-exchange market. The Treasury hypothesis was that dealers

73

would sell in an orderly manner and the pound would fall gently. Kit McMahon, the Bank's overseas director, warned the Treasury that the market was unstable and might not behave as civil servants and ministers thought it ought to. For his part, Richardson disliked the whole concept of manipulating the currency, but the Treasury persisted. A cut in minimum lending rate was scheduled for 5 March.

London had then (as it still has) the biggest foreign-exchange market in the world. It is, the Bank likes to think, the most professional and best run, but it has no physical centre at which deals are made: business is done on the telephone. The dealing room in the Bank is one of many in the City: it is functional and lived in. In 1976 it was lived in from 7.30 a.m. until 6.30 p.m., and sometimes much later than that. 'Those were soup and sandwich days,' recalls Graham Cocks, the Bank's chief foreign-exchange dealer.

The day most deeply etched in his memory is 4 March 1976. In the morning information began to filter in from commercial banks that a number of large orders for sterling was pushing its value up – the reverse of the Treasury's intention. The Bank's dealers reacted automatically and sold sterling, with the intention of holding down the rise in its value. But they were out of luck; at the moment they sold, the market price was brought down by a large sale of sterling by the Nigerian government. Bad luck was compounded by a confusion over strategy between the Bank and the Treasury. Lacking any signal from the Bank following its earlier sales of sterling, the commercial foreign-exchange dealers concluded that the policy was to force the rate down. Not wishing to hold a declining asset, they sold too. The pound began to fall. True, this is exactly what the Treasury did want, but the Bank was mortified. Having sold sterling first, it was vulnerable to the charge of insider trading – of having profited from private information. To make money by that kind of manipulation is the cardinal sin of central banking, and is supposed to happen only in banana republics.

Worse was to follow. The original strategy called for a reduction of M L R the following day, designed to make sterling slightly less attractive to foreign holders of pounds, whose sales would then bring the rate down gently. Richardson feared that, coming on top of the fall of sterling on 4 March, the reduction in M L R on 5 March would be taken by the markets as proof that the government's new policy was devaluation. But the reduction in M L R was already widely rumoured in the City, and the Chancellor argued that to cancel it would cause greater panic than letting it happen as planned.

The next day the markets noted the fall in MLR and duly panicked. Sterling fell below \$2.00 for the first time, and kept on falling. Within a week it was \$1.90, which would have pleased Treasury officials had it stopped there. But it went on down through the \$1.80s, and it was the Treasury's turn to panic. The Bank was told to move in to stop the fall at \$1.85, and the attempt to do so – by buying sterling in a falling market – cost \$1 billion. It was money ill spent, for by the beginning of June sterling stood at \$1.71. It was on the brink of collapse. Recriminations had also begun.

In the dissemination of information to journalists, the Treasury has a distinct advantage over the Bank. When it is necessary to protect itself from predators in the House of Commons, the Treasury can and will be absolutely vile, perpetrating every professional foul known to political man. Treasury spokesmen, briefing political reporters, boldly accused the Bank of lacking sufficient professionalism to carry out a straightforward exercise in market management. By the summer the Labour left was calling for Richardson's resignation. The Bank was accused by Tom Litterick, MP, and a number of others who signed a Commons motion, of deliberately starting a run on the pound to destabilize talks about incomes policy with the trade unions. Then the Prime Minister lent weight to the Treasury attack. James Callaghan, who had succeeded Harold Wilson in March 1976, accused the Bank of having forgotten its native skills: 'There used to be a man about fifteen years ago at the Bank who forecast exchange rates very accurately. But he has retired.' (He was referring to Roy Bridge, who was chief foreign-exchange adviser before the pound was floated, when forecasting was a good deal easier.) But the cruellest cut of all came from the other end of the political spectrum. Harold Macmillan said: 'The only people who have really speculated heavily in the pound are the Bank of England, and they've lost a great deal of money doing it. They'd better have stuck to bingo.'

The odious behaviour of the Treasury left the Bank temporarily speechless, and its public defence of itself was late and plaintive. Its spokesman denied that it had deliberately sold sterling in a falling market (the banana-republic option). 'We have never done it. Maybe we were too vigorous in stopping the pound rising, but that is quite different,' said Kit McMahon later. In the Bank's dealing room, the

Treasury's attacks were greeted with outrage: 'We'd have strangled anyone from the Treasury who came in here at that time,' Cocks said later. Disillusion set in quickly after that and a number of dealers left for jobs elsewhere in the City, for more money and less anguish.

The débâcle over sterling in the spring was only a harbinger of the real crisis. In June the Bank arranged a $5.3 billion standby loan from European central banks, and from the US Treasury and the Federal Reserve in Washington D C. With that sum in the reserves, the Bank intended to put a stop to speculation against the pound, once and for all. There was only one small hitch: the Americans had insisted that the loan be repaid in six months, which was the time they gave Callaghan's government to ease pressure on sterling by changing its economic policies, and, in particular, by cutting public expenditure. There were cuts in July, but the markets were not appeased, and when sterling began to fall again in September the Chancellor decided it was a waste to use the reserves any longer ($1.5 billion of the $5.3 billion loan had already been spent). Once the Bank stopped intervention, sterling went into further decline.

Throughout the spring and summer an objective of government policy had been to avoid asking for a long-term loan from the International Monetary Fund. This would mean the arrival of experts from Washington who would pick over Labour's economic policies, and state the conditions on which the money could be borrowed. It was an unpleasant business that took place in Portugal and Italy, but was not thought to be an appropriate way of conducting Her Majesty's Government. Labour's own way, on the other hand, was quite in-capable of inspiring confidence in foreign-exchange markets.

Almost a year earlier at the Mansion House, Richardson had spoken of the need for 'a mechanism of control over public expenditure which is effective in the short-run'. The I M F proved to be that mechanism. On 27 September the Chancellor and the Governor were due to fly out to Manila for the annual I M F/World Bank meeting, but as their limousine sped down the motorway to Heathrow Airport sterl-ing fell by $4\frac{1}{2}$ points. They turned back at the airport, and by the time Healey returned to Whitehall he had agreed to swallow the pill. An application was made to the I M F for a loan that would repay to the central banks the money that had already been drawn from the $5.3 standby loan of the previous June.

Many politicians lost any grip on reality during the three-month debate on the conditions attached to the IMF loan. Callaghan was concerned about the collapse of democracy in Britain; the Conservatives thought that in a consequent election they ought to be returned with a majority of 200; and the White House was fearful that Tony Benn was about to mount a coup inside the Labour Party. The argument inside the Cabinet was eventually resolved after ten weeks' hard labour on 15 December, with the announcement of a $3 billion cut in the Public Sector Borrowing Requirement over the next two years, and a promise to limit the expansion of domestic credit. In return, the government got its loan from the IMF, and an assurance that there would be enough money on standby in Basle to protect the pound against speculators while the Treasury and the Bank went about the orderly reduction in the international role of sterling. This standby loan was never called upon.

In the new year the credibility of sterling was miraculously restored, and the mood of the foreign-exchange markets shifted from depressive to manic. Politicians were confused but grateful and even the Bank admitted it had learned a valuable lesson about the volatility of international money markets. In fact, the 1976 sterling crisis had been a shattering experience with a number of important consequences for the future of the Bank and the Treasury.

The Bank had taken a beating when sterling fell in the spring, but by the end of the year its reputation was undergoing rehabilitation. It had been shown to be correct about the need to cut public spending, and right in suggesting that an IMF loan would end speculation against sterling. Richardson's judgement began to look good, not least to Denis Healey. One of the consequences of the crisis was the growth of the friendship between Healey and Richardson. The Chancellor's respect for the Governor increased as he discovered that they had a mutual respect for power, enjoyed exercising it and liked winning. 'They were both big men,' says Denzil Davies, who had become one of Healey's junior ministers. And both knew it.

The Treasury, on the other hand, had suffered a decline in its authority. In the Labour Party it was accused of having sold out socialism to the international bankers. The central bankers thought the Treasury was still a captive of the old Keynesian orthodoxy. In the relationship between the Treasury and the Bank there had been a noteworthy movement in the balance of power. In retrospect,

Richardson's most significant victory in 1976 was to persuade the Chancellor of the virtues of practical monetarism.

In the Mansion House speech on 21 October Healey stated that he had set a severe target for the money supply and boasted that he was the first British Chancellor to do so explicitly. The crisis created by the IMF, and public spending cuts, helped to obscure this statement but it meant that Healey had accepted that there was a link between heavy government borrowing and inflation; the government was beginning to take money seriously again, for the first time since the Second World War.

There had been controls on domestic credit expansion imposed by the IMF as a condition of an earlier loan in 1968, but these controls lapsed when the loan was repaid, and so did the Treasury's interest in money as a mechanism for controlling the level of growth in the economy. Charles Goodhart, the London School of Economics professor hired by the Bank to advise on monetary economics, wrote a number of papers about money in the late 1960s and early 1970s, but these were dismissed by most Treasury mandarins as impractical technical exercises. Anyway, the Treasury was Keynesian, and had little time for monetarism. They associated it with Milton Friedman, whom they dismissed as a fanatic.

Most of the Bank's economists were Keynesians too. John Fforde had been in the Bank many years, having been chief cashier in the 1960s, but before that he had been a don at Oxford, where Keynesian economics predominated. Kit McMahon was from the same stable. Christopher Dow, head of the economics department, had been at the Treasury and the Organization for Economic Cooperation and Development in Paris. He was steeped in Keynesianism, and although reticent of speech he was fluent on paper and contributed nobly to the many drafts of Richardson's speeches. Dow described economists as fools licensed to ask awkward questions, and Richardson took his questions seriously. Goodhart reports that the Governor treated his fool like a sage. Fforde's successor as chief cashier was John Page, and while he was not a man with any patience for theoretical speculation, when his advice was asked for he stood with Fforde and Dow.

The great reassessment began in 1976. Before then, the Keynesians in Threadneedle Street had taken Goodhart's contributions seriously without ever having been persuaded by them. It was Richardson who asked them to reconsider their assumptions about the value of targets for monetary aggregates, especially if they led to a reduction in government borrowing. They deduced that the Governor was picking up bad habits in Basle. Proof of this was provided by the gradual conversion to the concept of monetary targets of Kit McMahon, who also visited the Bank for International Settlements regularly. But the force of Richardson's argument had nothing to do with elegant exercises in economics.

One look at the rate of inflation in the British economy made it evident that Keynesian strategies were no longer working. The Keynesians did have one more strategem to urge – an incomes policy. This was a great favourite of Dow's, but the Governor's scepticism had begun to embrace incomes policy as well, for experience had demonstrated the inability of governments and trade unions to enforce it. By the summer of 1976 Richardson's instincts had persuaded him that another way of managing the economy must be tried. The first indication of this was characteristically roundabout and hedged with qualification. In a speech to the Chartered Institute of Public Finance and Accountancy in June 1976 he said:

> Incomes policy has proved valuable, but it would be foolish if
> we placed all our reliance on it. No one should, and I certainly do
> not, underestimate the continuing and direct relevance of prudent
> management of demand in the economy, including prudent monetary
> policy . . . There may be a case for expressing the rate of expenditure
> as envisaged by government in terms not of the increase of real
> output, but of the growth of money national income.

Money national income was a monetary aggregate. Increases in expenditure envisaged in terms of money aggregates were monetary targets.

In simple terms this meant: forget incomes policy, put demand management on one side, and look to monetary controls as the only practical means of attacking inflation. The message was intended for a particular audience comprising the Chancellor and his advisers, and within a month it was clear that Healey had received the communication. He announced that a target would be introduced for the money supply, and he was indeed the first British Chancellor explicitly to do so. The target he chose was M3, which is the sum of the deposits by British residents and companies in British banks.

For once, the Governor was ahead of nearly all his advisers.

John Fforde was not converted until September 1976. 'I threw in the towel then because we'd got ourselves in the position where we had to have an overriding constraint.' Dow later declared himself a great enthusiast for monetary targets, and contributed to the Governor's speeches that helped to make the idea respectable. In the Treasury there was a sense of defeat. Sir Douglas Wass regarded the business of monetary targets as highly suspect. He rationalized their adoption by noting that since the City took them seriously, they might stabilize the markets. But the phrase used by Wass and other Keynesians in the Treasury to describe this departure from Keynesianism was 'unbelieving monetarism'.

Richardson's enthusiasm for monetary targets did not mean that he had been converted to monetarism. Always a practical man, he sought a device which would shift the government's focus away from employment to inflation, and this was it. Practical monetarism was a political mechanism, although the Governor was not anxious to advertise this in 1976. A frank explanation of the reasons for it was eventually given by John Fforde, speaking to an audience of central bankers in New York in 1982.

> It would hardly have been possible to mount and carry through, over several years and without resort to direct controls of all kinds, so determined a counter-inflationary strategy if it had not been for the original 'political economy' of the firm monetary target. Though not considered at the time, it would have been possible to initiate such a strategy with a familiar 'Keynesian' exposition about managing demand downwards, and with greater consultation on ultimate objectives than on intermediate targets. But this would have meant disclosing objectives for, *inter alia*, output and employment. This would have been a very hazardous exercise, and the objectives would either have been unacceptable to public opinion or else inadequate to secure a substantial reduction in the rate of inflation, or both. Use of strong intermediate targets for money supply and government borrowing enabled the authorities to stand back from output and employment as such and to stress the vital part to be played in respect of these by the trend of industrial costs. In short, whatever the subsequent difficulties of working with intermediate targets, they were vitally important at the outset in order to signal a decisive break with the past and enable the authorities to set out with presentational confidence upon a relatively uncharted sea.

The fact that one certain outcome of the policy would be significantly higher unemployment than at any time since the Depression could be glossed over. 'Presentational confidence' means not having to talk about the disagreeable side-effects of the policy.

However it was presented, practical monetarism enhanced the economic role of the markets in the City of London. This was demonstrated in the summer of 1977 when sterling, revitalized by the IMF loan, began to rise in value, making British exports more costly. The interest rate is the simple tool designed to correct this difficulty. Bring down interest rates and the exchange rate will come down. As any Labour Chancellor always had, Healey did just this. The consequence, however, was that lower interest rates increased bank borrowing, and M3 went up beyond the target range that Healey had set for it. The choice was clear: industry or markets? Exports or money supply? Healey's decision was to increase the interest rate so as to bring down bank lending and the increase in M3. The markets won, and when they began to doubt Labour's good intentions again in 1978, the signal from the Treasury was the same: it was intended to adhere to the M3 target, though on this occasion it deployed the old-fashioned remedy of applying 'the corset' to impose controls on bank lending.

After two generations during which the markets had been regarded as old-fashioned, they mattered again. Since markets are the central bank's particular area of expertise, its own importance was increased. The Bank was again in the forefront of economic policy-making and Richardson relished his position as spokesman for practical monetarism, though the act of putting the idea down on paper immediately diluted it. Richardson's speeches reflected 'a collectivity' – as he called it – inside the Bank, which meant that they embraced various shades in the spectrum of economic analysis.

The Governor's most important speech was the inaugural Mais Lecture at the City University in February 1978. This relied heavily on contributions from both Dow and Goodhart, and contained masterpieces of Richardsonspeak, such as: 'We hope to be sensitive to new currents of thought; yet at the same time we must exercise our judgement and not be too ready to accept every change of intellectual fashion. It is, however, reasonable to expect us to seek to abstract ourselves from day-to-day pressures and to try to systematize the philosophy that underlies our actions, though of course I have no illusions that I am stating the last word.'

He was careful to affirm the virtues of demand management ('to eschew it entirely would involve tenacious faith in the self-correcting properties of the private sector of the economy'). But, like blue sky appearing through the clouds, the message eventually shone through: 'Though the causation may not be simple, there is an observable statistical relation between monetary growth and the pace of inflation . . . A great deal of work has been devoted to the study of the relationship over long time periods in many countries; and that there is such a relationship cannot, I think, be doubted.'

There were economists left who questioned an automatic relationship between money supply and inflation. But most laymen agreed with Richardson; what he said seemed obvious sense. There were undercurrents of criticism, but they were directed more at the Bank's methods, not its judgement. Rupert Pennant-Rea, who worked for Dow during this period before joining the *Economist* (he later became its editor), was no follower of Friedman at that time, but he regarded the reintroduction of an outmoded device like 'the corset' as intellectual fraud: 'If they want monetarism, let's have it, not a muddled compromise.' Monetarists like Alan Walters, getting a hearing from the Opposition under Mrs Thatcher, disapproved of the confusion about the ultimate objectives of financial policy. His charge was that the Bank talked monetarism, but was not really interested in applying it – that it was only pretending. Of course, Walters was right. For monetarists like him, the theory was an end in itself, and its application was intended to usher in a revolution in economic management. Central bankers do not like revolutions of any kind and, for men like Richardson, monetarism was a means to an end designed to open up the battle against inflation.

This difference in approach to monetarism was to cause Richardson much grief before his governorship ended, but it hardly mattered at all in 1977. On 26 January 1978, Gordon Richardson was reappointed for a second term. Because it was taken for granted, the announcement was hardly noticed. He had by that time established himself as the country's central banker. Denzil Davies, the junior minister at the Treasury, noted that Richardson even looked like a central banker: 'The nose has a lot to do with it.' (Prominence equals authority?) Richardson's story of the secondary banking crisis, told in the House of Commons in January 1978 and the Mais Lecture the following month, attracted more attention from the newspapers than he had received before. He was clearly a man to be reckoned with. And when that is true of the Governor it is true of the Bank of England.

Later in the year I interviewed Richardson. He saw me alone in the Governor's room: hair, silver; suit, dark grey and double-breasted; handshake, firm; eyes, dark blue; gaze, piercing. Perhaps because I was writing for an American magazine, he agreed to be quoted (one of the few occasions on which he did), and since his conversation reflected the mood of the Bank at the time, it is worth recalling. I started by quoting Bagehot, on the relationship between the Bank and the government: 'I confess I believe that this varies very much with the character of the Governor for the time being. A strong Governor does much mainly on his own responsibility, and a weak Governor does little.' Richardson considered carefully before saying that he was not sure this particular dichotomy was the best test of strength and weakness.

'I could think of a number of areas in which the Governor might be doing a lot on his own, and not deploying his strength. It depends on the circumstances. His vital role is his independent contribution to economic policy, especially in monetary affairs and exchange-rate policy, and then its execution. It's a hard thing to determine the degree of influence and persuasiveness, but that is the index of his strength. In the area of banking supervision, that responsibility is not shared, and that would satisfy Bagehot's definition, but I don't find his proposition all that illuminating and interesting today. I don't feel the sharp divide.'

What interested the Governor was the number of changes the Bank had made in the last five years. 'One of the things that strikes me most clearly is that a central bank should be stable and solid, but it shouldn't be static.' Some of the changes had been involuntary, like those forced on it by the fringe-banking crisis, and he admitted that not everything the Bank did was exempt from criticism. 'If you get something on that scale you don't expect every action to be perfect. It's like being a general in charge of a division. There are clouds of smoke and the information is imperfect; the decisions he takes then might be different from the decisions he would take at leisure with more information.' But Richardson's battle reminiscences were those of a victorious general.

I was especially interested in his use of the word 'stable', because it seemed to me then that stability was the ultimate ambition of the men who run the Bank; they stubbornly refused to conform to the instability they saw around them, whether they were running the printing works, keeping the banks in order, observing some eccentricities of economic policy, or even seeing that a building was spick and span.

This was, perhaps, why the Bank appeared old-fashioned and not representative of contemporary Britain. Richardson felt not the slightest compulsion to apologize. 'I *do* like the notion of the Bank being orderly. I wouldn't like to think of that word as oppressive. Order is liberating, not repressive.' I wondered if he thought the stability of the Bank was not the exception rather than the rule. 'It's no use pretending that there haven't been changes in Britain,' he replied, 'but nobody is going to tell me that ordinary British people don't reflect the standards I'm talking about.'

5

A Law to Separate Sheep from Goats

When a new division of banking supervision was set up in the autumn of 1974, George Blunden was the obvious man to run it. As a second-generation Bank man, he was fiercely proud of its reputation. His standards were high, and any employee who failed to meet them was dressed down, sharply. Although his hair was white, and he was not many years away from retirement, Blunden was still forceful and energetic.

Like many veterans of the Bank, Blunden was not particularly sympathetic to the concept of bank supervision. Apart from an old-fashioned belief that the bank customer – like the buyer – should beware, he observed that most attempts to supervise banks came after a disaster, and was not keen to be the man responsible for shutting the stable door too late. But it was clear to him early in 1974, when the secondary banking crisis was still unravelling, that the markets in London were nervous and needed soothing. Moreover, the authority of the Bank had to be reinforced. Jim Keogh, the former principal of the discount office, may have been privately identified as the scapegoat and have gone off to Singapore, but the City still wanted the Bank to be seen to be doing something. Since the City was not quite sure what, Blunden had room for manoeuvre.

The principal of the discount office had never been referred to as a bank supervisor. Rather, he had established 'close liaison' with banks and acceptance houses. He was the Bank's official gossip, whose job was to lunch with directors and partners of clearing banks and merchant banks. When something appeared to be out of line with the unwritten rules of the community, he had direct access to the Governor, who might be called upon to raise his eyebrow in disapproval.

The only reference to this responsibility in the law was a couple of sentences in section 4 of the Bank of England Act 1946, enabling the discount office 'to request information from and make recommendations to bankers', and, if necessary, and with the consent of the Treasury, 'to issue directions to any bankers for the purpose of securing that effect is given to any such request or recommendation'.

As for the definition of 'banker', it was a circumlocutory masterpiece of the parliamentary draftsman's art. A banker was 'any such person carrying on a banking undertaking as may be declared by the Treasury to be a banker for the purpose of this section'. About the definition of a bank, however, the Act was totally silent. Consequently, a bank was a bank when the Bank declared it was a bank. Gordon

Richardson echoed this tradition of inexact definition when he told colleagues that as far as he was concerned banks were like elephants: you recognized one when you saw it. The Bank's vision was in fact strictly limited, and the banks it recognized were the clearing banks and the merchant houses whose credit was good enough to allow them accounts at the Bank of England, and whose bills were discounted by the Bank at the best rate. Another mark of approval was a licence to deal in foreign exchange.

Of course, there were other institutions taking deposits that did not have the familiar outline of an elephant. These were not the responsibility of the Bank at all, since they were defined under section 123 of the Companies Act, which was administered by the Department of Trade. Once licensed they were exempt from the Money Lenders Acts, but little else, and they became known as 'section 123 banks'. They constituted the secondary or fringe banking system.

The implication of the secondary banking crisis was that the Bank could no longer ignore these second- and third-division players. Indeed, Blunden could not wait until the law had been changed to recognize the Bank's wider responsibilities. He had been provided with a text for his work by Richardson in February 1974, when the Governor said that traditional systems of self-regulation and self-discipline could be put to too great a test if competition from the less-regulated and less-disciplined was too easily permitted. Richardson did not intend that supervision should get out of hand. As *The Times* reported: 'He saw no need to rush into some "elaborate statutory system of supervision which might only succeed in appearing to render trouble unlikely at the expense of initiative".' In fact, Richardson did not believe that statutory supervision of 'proper banks' – the elephant-shaped banks – was necessary at all.

That debate would have to wait, however. The City was in a dreadful state of agitation about the secondary banking crisis, and at the height of the summer of 1974 the clearing banks and the Bank of England had committed £1,200 million – a sum that amounted to 40 per cent of the total reserves of the English and Scottish clearers – to combat the banking crisis. They were anxious to know when it might end and how it would be prevented from happening again, and Blunden's immediate task was to demonstrate that the Bank understood the fears of the City and, indeed, of the Treasury.

The earliest proposals looked as if they were merely cosmetic:

Blunden recommended the establishment of a new department of banking and money-market supervision to take over from the discount office. But there was more to it than the introduction of the word 'supervision' for the first time in a departmental title. By divorcing the responsibility from the chief cashier's office and by sharply increasing the number of supervisory staff (although it was said in the City that only one member of the department had any commercial banking experience), the Bank was acknowledging that in future the concept would be taken much more seriously. The larger staff began to apply a new standard known as the risk–asset ratio to bank borrowing (this related the risk of losses inherent in the assets of the business to the capital available to cover such losses). Principles were set out for foreign-exchange dealing, and banks were expected to provide much fuller statistical returns and to submit themselves to questioning by supervisors about the content of the balance-sheet. The clearers were, however, exempt from this inquisitorial examination; 'a relaxed two-way exchange' was sufficient for the clearing and merchant banks.

Further evidence of the intentions of the Bank came in November 1974, when a committee of supervisors from ten leading industrial nations was created at a meeting in Basle of the Bank for International Settlements. The spur was the collapse of the Bankhaus Herstatt in Frankfurt the previous June, and the committee – known at first as the Blunden Committee after its first chairman – quickly established a principle for international banking supervision: that of parental responsibility. This meant that the prudent management of branches of a British bank, wherever they were, would be the responsibility of British supervisors. American supervisors would be ultimately responsible for, say, the London branch of Citibank. This concentrated the minds of top managers in the clearing banks, and created a kind of work inside the Bank that had never been done before.

By 1975 the Bank had thoroughly reorganized its system of bank supervision, and the secondary banks that had survived the crisis were no longer at risk. If the Bank had had its own way change would have stopped there. But there were compelling reasons for legislating to regulate banks properly. Unable to resist these, the Bank was determined that any Banking Bill should contain nothing untoward to upset the 'proper' part of the banking industry. With one hand the Bank established a regulatory system. With the other it was about to argue that statutory enforcement would be pernicious. It was a puzzling business.

The idea of statutory banking supervision was not new. Britain was a member of the European Economic Community and the passion for harmonization that gripped the Eurocrats made it inevitable that there would be a binding directive about banks. Discussions had begun in 1972 (with a member of the chief cashier's department named Frank Hall representing the Bank as an observer) and it was soon evident that any organization that took deposits or lent money would have to satisfy some public authority of the competence and integrity of its management and the soundness of its balance-sheet. That European rule would apply not only to section 123 banks; it would apply to the likes of NatWest and Barclays too. Furthermore, the European Commission's discussions reflected a growing concern that depositors should be protected (consumer protection had become a fashionable issue in British politics) and 'Europeanism' reflected a belief that rules were more effective when they were written down, rather than handed down as was the City's way.

The Bank of England rarely thought of banking in terms of individual customers and was not enthusiastic about either consumerism or rule-making; neither was thought relevant to British banking. The whole point of the secondary banking crisis, according to the Bank, was that no depositor lost money. As for rules, the Bank took it for granted that the Governor's authority was more effective than written instructions.

Despite new language, more supervisors and tougher standards, the Bank in 1975 still believed that supervision was a personal matter. As Blunden said: 'Frequent discussions between senior managers of banks and senior officials of the Bank of England are more conducive to the maintenance of good banking practices than the technique adopted in many other countries of sending in teams of inspectors to examine the bank's books.' And Richardson's view echoed this: 'It is much more useful to seek to influence a bank's policy from the top than to try to monitor its procedures from the bottom.' Bank supervisors, however, were not convinced. John Roper, a senior supervisor, recalls that if merchant banks took exception to criticism from the Bank's supervisors, they would complain to the deputy governor. The word would then come down from the Governor: 'Soft pedal, please'.

The intention to legislate was formally announced in November

1975 by a Treasury civil servant giving evidence to the parliamentary select committee examining the legal implications of E E C directives. But the E E C was, in fact, only a pretext. Labour ministers at the Treasury were keen to extend consumer protection to the banks' customers, and to deal with the flaws that the secondary banking crisis had revealed. The real debate now was about who should supervise and with what powers. There was a suggestion that the secondary banks should be supervised by the Department of Trade and Industry, but Richardson quickly scotched that. *The Times* reported a speech he made in Luxemburg that November: the Bank of England, he said, was unquestioningly accepted as the institution responsible for banking supervision in the United Kingdom, but this was not a role that derived from specific statutory authority. 'I trust that it will be possible to preserve within the new statutory framework the valuable features of our present philosophy and approach to the supervision of banks, while giving the authorities greater powers over deposit-taking institutions.'

In fact, Richardson's assertion that the Bank was the only organization capable of supervision was not unquestioningly accepted within the Bank itself. For instance, Christopher Dow, the distinguished head of the economics department, sensed potential danger in a statutory supervisory role. For a start, it was different from the Bank's traditional Olympian role in the markets. Disagreements could become the subject of litigation, which could harm the Bank's authority, he argued. 'Keep a buffer between you and the clients' was Dow's rule. He thought that banking supervision ought to be undertaken by an authority independent of both the Bank and the Treasury. Dow recalls that when Richardson was uncertain about a decision he would usually organize a meeting of his advisers. But on the subject of banking supervision there were no such meetings at all. 'I never got a look in,' says Dow. 'The Governor had made up his mind.'

Blunden made the same discovery, quite independently, when he also asked Richardson whether an option might be to dispose of the supervisory responsibility. 'Not on,' was Richardson's crisp response. So Blunden, along with John Fforde, set about designing a system that would satisfy the need for legislation without compromising the Bank's traditional relationships. The result was a two-tier system of supervision.

Its objective was to distinguish between 'proper banks' and

secondary banks, a group that became known as licensed deposit takers, or LDTs. To qualify for the top tier, a bank had to provide either a wide range of banking services or a specialized banking service. This imperfect definition was intended to lend top-tier status to merchant banks even though it might also be reasonably applied to a solicitor investing a widow's mite. This potential confusion was resolved by the Bank in its most magisterial manner: 'Any question whether an institution is to be regarded as providing at any time either a wide range of banking services or a highly specialized banking service shall be determined by the Bank.'

As a means of giving the Governor his own way, the two-tier system was a clever expedient, but its flaws were apparent almost immediately, especially to the experts in the banking supervision department and the few specialists in the Treasury. There was a case to be made for the two-tier system, of course, and it was expressed on behalf of the Bank by Frank Hall, the man who had sat through the early discussions in Brussels about authorizing banks and who had a major involvement in the subsequent White Paper and legislation. (He joined the Treasury team responsible for the preparation of the Banking Bill and he helped to draft much of it.) Hall justified the two-tier system in the perspective of that time like this:

> The way we actually approached it was to ask whether there was a difference between the sort of response we could expect from, say, Barclays on the one hand and a small firm of solicitors re-lending on second mortgages on the other. Between Barclays and the Bank there is a continuity of shared interests, but to many firms of solicitors the Bank is for practical purposes an unknown concept. The Bank might tell them what to do, and they might say 'What is your authority?' Then we can reply: 'The Banking Act.'

Hall was speaking to a brief, and was not wholly committed to the two-tier system himself. Some of his colleagues were even more sceptical, particularly those who would have to apply the new law. Some were totally opposed to the two-tier division. John Roper, a veteran manager in the banking-supervision department, says: 'What we didn't believe in, from a very senior level downwards, was the two-tier system. Who were we to pour British banks into a mould? It was artificial and wrong.' When Roper expressed his doubts to superiors in the Bank, the reaction was blunt: 'Who asked you?' is the way he recalls it. Other colleagues were concerned about the distinction they were being asked to draw between top- and second-tier banks. Tony Nicolle, another senior supervisor at the Bank, observed: 'The people who instituted the system had no conception of what it would be like to apply it. Since it was possible that the line dividing the two tiers had been drawn in the wrong place, you could never apply it properly.' At the Treasury, some civil servants working in the home-finance division – which was formally responsible for the contents of the Bill – shared the doubts of the professional supervisors. But this debate was not decided by professionals in the Bank or at the Treasury: Gordon Richardson carried the argument right to the top in 1976.

He cared enough about the two-tier system to ask the Chancellor to override his officials, and Denis Healey cared enough about his relationship with the Governor not to wish to start a quarrel with him, especially in the early summer of 1976, when the sterling crisis was brewing. The Treasury had borrowed heavily from a group of central banks in June 1976, and Healey was anxious to keep Richardson on his side. If the Governor were to cast doubt on the government's policies, his central-banking colleagues might get cold feet. It was no time to contradict Richardson on a technical matter that had no detectable political repercussions. When the White Paper appeared in August 1976 it outlined the basic features of a two-tier system of banking supervision, as Richardson had requested.

This was not an unqualified victory for the Bank. Michael Bridgeman, the home-finance chief, remembers: 'There were two debates: about the two-tier system, and the extent to which the top tier had any statutory supervision at all. The Bank won the first, but the Treasury won the second.' In line with the European directive, the top tier would have to meet the conditions of authorization by the Bank, and the proposals in the White Paper curbed the Bank's discretion to define the status of a bank. Objective criteria for admission into the top tier were to be included in the Bill. One other proposal was included that the Bank had opposed: there would be a Depositors' Protection Fund, after all.

But the argument did not end in August 1976, partly because Denzil Davies had been appointed the Treasury's new junior minister. He confessed that he knew little about banking, but he was expert on the law, and he did not like what he read in the draft legislation. He did a quick study of the American alternative to the British system of banking supervision, which relies heavily on a formal inspection system backed by volumes of legal precedent. He was not persuaded by that, but he was not keen on the Bank's alternative either. 'It seemed to me that the two-tier system was rubbish, and that the Bank's reasons for wanting it were mystical. Exempting the first division of banks from proper supervision didn't seem to make any sense, and I couldn't see how it would work. I tried to get it changed, and went as far as Denis Healey, but he wasn't interested. I was only a junior man, and I couldn't argue with the Governor. Frankly, he won hands down.' (Davies remembers a warning from Charles Williams – now Lord Williams – one of the few merchant bankers in the City who overtly supported Labour, that it was mistaken to make the Bank the supervisory authority in the first place. 'I told him I thought he was probably right, but that there was no way I was going to fight the Bank and win.')

While Davies conceded defeat in the main battle, he fought a few other skirmishes with the Bank in which he was not always the loser. Sir Jasper Hollom, the deputy governor, would arrive at the Treasury for regular bouts with Davies, who asked, one day, to which authority a disgruntled banker, faced with the prospect of being declared a licensed deposit taker instead of a top-tier man, could appeal.

'The Bank,' Hollom replied.

'According to what criteria?' Davies asked.

'The Bank's,' said Hollom.

Davies asked where these criteria would be published.

'In the *Bank of England Quarterly Bulletin*,' Hollom replied.

'Not good enough,' said Davies. He wanted judicial arbitration by the courts. The Bank then dug up an obscure case in Irish law in which the judge had made a mess of some banking business, and used it to argue that the courts were not competent to judge banking business – an uncommonly untactful move by Hollom, since Davies was a lawyer. Eventually Hollom accepted that a tribunal system would hear appeals from disgruntled bankers who had been consigned to LDT status.

The definition of a bank proved exceptionally difficult to arrive at, once the old formula that a bank was what the Bank recognized as a bank was no longer accepted. The final definition included a string of words containing value judgements, like 'high reputation and standing in the financial community', 'integrity and prudence', 'professional skills' and so on. The looser the definition, the better pleased the Bank was.

Davies ended his negotiations with Hollom having drawn two conclusions about the Bank of England: first, that the Bank was convinced it always knew best, and, second, that the authority of the Governor was as all-pervasive as it was said to be. 'It was a problem getting anything out of the Bank at all, especially on paper. Sir Jasper was a nice guy, but the impression I got was that nothing was ever decided in the Bank until the Governor had pronounced.' And when the Governor did pronounce in the late 1970s, he usually had his way.

For Davies, if not the Bank, the most significant item in the Banking Bill was the Depositors' Protection Fund, which guarantees 75 per cent of the first £10,000 in a customer's account should his or her bank fail. Indeed, Davies's speech in the House of Commons reflected this emphasis when he began: 'This Bill has a single objective, and that is the protection of depositors.' The Commons accepted the argument, and hardly any members cared how many tiers there were to be in the new system of banking supervision. No trouble there, but Davies did have opposition to his plans for depositor protection. The Fund brought him into conflict with the clearing banks which dominated the top tier of the system and which began lobbying in Whitehall and Westminster in 1978. That does not sound unusual, but there was more to it than met the eye, for it marked a shift in the relationship between the Bank and the clearing banks.

Despite the valiant battle the Bank had fought on their behalf to minimize the amount of supervision they would be subjected to, the clearers no longer accepted uncritically the contention that the Bank represented all their interests to the government. Since successive Governors had argued that this representative capacity of the Bank – speaking for the City in Whitehall – was one function that differentiated the Bank from other nationalized industries and validated its independence from government, the charge that it was incapable of performing the role was a blow, if true. In the history of the Banking Act, this may appear to be no more than a footnote. In the recent history of the Bank, however, its significance is somewhat greater.

Nationalization in 1946 had had little effect on the relationship between the Bank and the clearing banks. Mostly, they conformed when the Governor raised his eyebrow, and while the Bank rationed the amount that banks could lend before 1971, it never had to threaten in order to have its way. When the banking industry wanted to say something to government it used proper channels, and chairmen of the clearing banks trooped in to see the Governor (or chief executives sought out the chief cashier) to ask him to pass on the message.

The relationship had been subjected to strain during the secondary banking crisis, when the clearers had put up hundreds of millions of pounds on the understanding that the Bank was going to recycle the money. But in 1975, and especially in the cases of Slater Walker and Edward Bates, the problem was no longer one of liquidity merely, but of solvency. Those banks were bust, and the Bank was intent on bailing them out. The clearers wanted nothing to do with that. Then there was the unhappy memory of the Consumer Credit Act 1974. That Bill had contained an item which forced all lenders to state the exact rate of interest a borrower was paying. The intention was to protect consumers from exorbitant rates of interest in hire-purchase agreements, but as the Bill passed through Parliament the banks suddenly grasped that it would also apply to them, and that all overdrafts would have to state the interest the customer was paying. The cost in manpower would be enormous (and customers would finally realize how it was that banks made such profits). The clearers looked to the Bank to obtain their exclusion from this imposition, but the Bank, slow to grasp the implications, failed to deliver. It was a technical matter, and the clearers blamed the chief cashier, John Page. 'The Bank showed itself insensitive to the changes of the previous decade,' says Ian Morison, then head of research for the Committee of London Clearing Banks.

In retrospect, senior managers at the Bank conceded the truth of this. David Somerset, who was a deputy chief cashier in the 1970s, says of the Consumer Credit Act:

> We probably didn't understand the full implications of it. Because we didn't know enough about retail banking, we simply couldn't act as a conduit. We had begun to lose the confidence of the City, where it was generally being said that it was no use relying on the Bank to talk to Whitehall because it didn't do it frightfully well. Westminster began to encourage these links. People went straight to a minister, and sometimes it worked, so people tried again.

Consequently, when the Depositors' Protection Fund appeared in the Banking Bill, the clearing banks did not waste time looking for help from the Bank. 'Before long the Treasury was asking us to lunch,' said Ian Morison.

Denzil Davies's commitment to depositor protection gave the clearers little hope of removing the Fund from the Bill altogether (although they argued cleverly that if the new supervisory function worked properly there would be no need for depositor protection). But they hectored and snapped at the Treasury, and, in doing so, discovered that they had transformed themselves into a political pressure group.

The Banking Bill was passed through the Commons in the winter of 1978–9, and was still waiting to be heard in the Lords when the government lost a vital vote of confidence. If the Bill were to become law before the dissolution of Parliament prior to the 1979 General Election, it would have to be rushed through the Lords. At last the clearing banks were in a position to use their brand new political influence. Those peers who also held directorships of banks let the Treasury know that the price of their support was the end of the requirement to show the rate of interest on bank statements. The amendment was proposed and passed in a day – a result the Bank had been powerless to achieve.

Although the parliamentary debates had proved amicable, three statements are worth recording.

Lord McClusky, opening the second reading debate in the Lords:

> The Banking Bill is designed to preserve as much as possible
> of the flexible approach which the Bank of England has brought over
> the years to the supervision of the primary banking sector.

Ian Stewart, MP for Hitchin, in the Commons:

> It would be fair to say that the success of the Bill and the
> system it will establish will owe a great deal to the way the parties
> to it carry out their various responsibilities, duties and functions; not
> least the Bank of England.

Sir Peter Tapsell, MP:

> Harmonization is the enemy of informality. The ultimate
> significance of codification for the future role of the Bank of England
> may, I suspect, prove to be the most significant effect of the new
> Bill.

The Banking Act received the royal assent on 4 April 1979, the last day of the session before the General Election that took Mrs Margaret Thatcher to Downing Street. In Threadneedle Street, the number two in banking supervision was now a man named Tony Coleby, and he remembers the debate within the Bank at the time: 'What moved Gordon Richardson was the feeling that the status attaching to the word "bank" was one which could be mistaken if applied to lesser institutions, and might mislead the public about those institutions. A few of us were, perhaps, more conscious than he was of the problems that would result from the two-tier system – because of the implied separation of the sheep and the goats. I hoped it would not be a permanent arrangement and privately gave it ten years. What was necessary was that we got to grips with the licensed deposit takers and either made them capable bankers, or deprived them of the right to be bankers at all. We should aim to achieve sufficient confidence after ten years that we had done so to be able to dispense with any need to categorize banks in two tiers.'

That assessment was to prove shrewd in every respect except the time scale.

6

Operating in a Stylish Way

By 1979 Gordon Richardson had carefully constructed an image for the Bank that was based upon the appearance of effortless superiority. This impression that the Bank knew best made enemies for it among Labour politicians like Denzil Davies. After four years in the Treasury he decided that the Bank of England was not necessary at all and that its essential function in the domestic and international money markets could be performed by a Treasury under-secretary and a small team of civil servants. James Callaghan never forgave the Bank for the confusion and humiliation that preceded the IMF loan. But Richardson retained sufficient authority to win battles between the Bank and the Treasury, and, despite the new coolness of the clearing banks, his statements were taking on an oracular tone. He had begun to cut a figure in public; this was Richardson in his prime.

Inside the Bank it was understood that changes were occurring in everything it did, but it remained proud of its traditional qualities. By 1979 Kit McMahon, who was born in Australia and recruited from Oxford, had become overseas director, and when I talked to him he identified the changes that had occurred in his fifteen years at the Bank. 'When I came here we were in the final stages of defending the fixed value of sterling, and the Bank was ill-equipped to envisage the changes that were coming. It was rather an emotional place then, and merely to mention devaluation was like saying a four-letter word in church. It is difficult to appreciate how much things have changed since then. People could see that sterling was going to wind down, but no one could have guessed the speed of it. I think the Bank retains a certain mystique abroad, though it has suffered with the decline of sterling: the Bank stood for that part of Britain which has taken a beating. But it is technically admired. We are still operating in a stylish way.'

The question was, could it cope with further changes and continue to operate in the same way? About some things there was no choice. One little-publicized activity was, and is, registering the owners of government stock and paying dividends twice a year. This is one of the original activities of the Bank of England, and the registrar's department was established in 1694. The departmental archives, housed in a neo-Georgian building on the sportsground at Roehampton, are, *inter alia*, one of the best autograph collections in Britain. One entry dated 16 November 1759 is signed by George and Martha Washington (their dividends were sequestered when the Revolution began). Recently, the present registrar, Gair Drake, took out at

100

random a register for $2\frac{1}{2}$ per cent annuities and within ten minutes found the signature of William Pitt. Behind his desk hang powers of attorney signed by Nelson. One of the Victorian paintings in the anteroom leading to the parlours is Frith's 'Dividend Day at the Bank of England', because in the Soane bank the job was still done in Threadneedle Street. When the department expanded it had to move to Finsbury Circus. After the Second World War there was no longer room there either, and the department was eventually housed in a dull post-war development called New Change on one of the finest sites in Britain, overlooking St Paul's Cathedral from the east. In New Change there was a staff of 2,200 clerks and managers – two thirds of them women – keeping the accounts in looseleaf books. Automation began in the early 1960s, when records of three million annual payments were put on punched cards.

The manager in charge of computers in the registrar's department now is Mike Lees, who was one of the original programmers for the first generation of I C L computers. Lees had joined the Bank after national service and he was assigned to computer work in the registrar's department because of his height. Two tall men were needed to look for missing styluses on the printers used in the production of interest warrants (these styluses were positioned six feet above the ground). Not long after this Lees came in even more useful, for he had a natural aptitude for computer programming. He had been chosen to learn the trade with I C T (I C L), back in the primitive days of the commercial application of computer science, twenty-five years ago. There were no specialists: 'You were a computer man. You did the analysis, wrote the program, and tested it until you were ready to go. I don't think I consciously did systems analysis. I just wrote a chart of what we were trying to do.'

The Bank was one of the first institutional customers for computers, and its experts were all home-grown: 'We were a small group, seen as rather aloof. We were all so fiendishly interested.' Originally, government stock registers were held on some forty reels of magnetic tape that had to be checked and maintained each night. But management in the registrar's department was bold, the Governor was helpful, and I C L was asked to put the whole sequence from registering ownership to paying dividends on to an on-line system, giving each operator access to the stock registers via a visual display unit on the desk. That went live in 1975, and two years later an index of four

101

million stock-holders had been prepared (since updated to include postcodes). Lees confesses that the system is not absolutely perfect – there are two or three computer-induced mistakes a year (usually due to random hammer failures on the printer). In less exacting circumstances, this counts as a nil error rate. 'As registrar for British government securities we ought to set an exemplary standard,' remarks Lees. Thus speaks an old Bank man.

Computerization has radically altered the character of the registrar's department. Staff numbers have fallen from 2,200 to 900, of whom one in six are well-paid data programmers and computer operators. (In this area the Bank ignores its own wage structure and pays market rates.) The ratio of men to women has shifted to 50:50, and except for the minority playing sport at Roehampton, the Bank is hardly distinguishable from any other employer in the City. It is difficult to program mystique.

The changes in the registrar's department were voluntary, but this was not always the case, and the origin of the numerous obligatory changes was in 1969, when the House of Commons select committee on nationalized industries began to poke around in the affairs of the Bank. In Threadneedle Street, the first response was to dismiss the work of the committee as a gross impertinence, based on the dismal misconception that the Bank was a nationalized *industry*. This response made it an even more tempting target for Labour politicians like Ian Mikardo. The raw material was wonderfully rich. For instance, the Bank of England never published accounts. Not even the Treasury knew how much profit it made, and the annual dividend paid to the government was decided privately by the Governor and the deputy governor. Since there were no outside constraints on the numbers of people employed by the Bank, staffing policy was as generous as in first class on an ocean liner. John Rumins, the Bank's financial controller, who was hired from Coopers and Lybrand in 1972, was shocked: 'The Bank was opulent,' he recalls.

In 1972 the Commons select committee recommended sweeping changes, and the Treasury adopted many of its proposals with an eagerness which made it clear in Threadneedle Street that there were no allies in Whitehall. For the Treasury, it was a wonderful opportunity to pay off old scores, and it did so with some finesse. To establish access to the Bank's private budget-making process, the Treasury produced the argument that it was quite wrong for government to expect the

Bank to perform services for its agencies without charging. It offered
to pay the Bank for the management of British government stocks,
the exchange equalization account, exchange control and the note
issue. All the Treasury would ask in return was good value for its
money: the corollary meant the end of private accounting, there being
no way of proving the Bank's efficiency to the Treasury without revealing its cost structure.

The next requirement was that the Bank should declare a profit.
The Treasury saw no reason why the Bank should retain profit to build
up its private reserves – Whitehall thought the Bank did not need
reserves – and demanded that the government be paid a larger dividend. This sum was called 'the agreed provision'. Predictably, there
was no agreement about the provision and a dog-fight went on for
twelve years until 1984, before the two sides declared a draw. 'Eventually, everyone got fed up with the argument,' says Rumins, a participant in this annual affray. The settlement provided for the profits
to be split equally: the Bank would retain half for reserves; the rest
would be paid to the Treasury as a dividend.

The staff felt the full impact of the new arrangement first. By
1974 the Treasury had become interested in public-expenditure cuts,
and the Bank was no longer immune from such disagreeable exercises.
When the deputy governor, Sir Jasper Hollom, announced that cuts
were proposed, Rumins remembers the reaction: 'Everyone thought it
was a game.' Sir Jasper played for real by announcing across-the-
board percentage cuts in staff levels, and then he handed the task to
George Blunden: 'A hard-nosed analyst who got after the numbers,'
says Rumins. Hollom and Blunden were determined to make the Bank
more efficient, but there was a price to pay.

Gentlemen of the Bank of England were not expected to complain
about their wages and conditions, though this had not always prevented them from doing so. In 1919 a vintage memorandum had been
sent by the staff to the Court complaining that after four and a half
years of war, when 'the human element in Bank life has been unfortunately too little accounted for, there is bound to be a reaction
accompanied by unrest, dissatisfaction and yearning for better conditions of hours and pay'. But that was the exception, not the rule.
The gentlemen did not complain, and the players were disinclined to do
so for reasons outlined by an official of the staff association: 'The Bank
attracted a very conservative, working-class person who wanted to

own a house. They got benefits that weren't available in outside industry, so they moaned and groaned, but the housing loan kept them
anchored at the Bank.'

For thirty years after the Second World War the Bank's wages
and conditions (loans for housing, private education and commuter
travel) reflected a determination to recruit and retain staff at a high
level. Civil servants and employees of the clearing banks were left some
way behind until the mid-1970s, when the clearers began to catch up.
Soon the Bank of England Staff Organization (BESO) was complaining
that the clearers were not only offering London allowances, but profit
sharing, productivity bonuses, and even, for senior managers, cars.

BESO declared its independence in 1976, when it left the Bank's
premises and took offices 150 yards down Queen Victoria Street. The
general secretary then was a graduate from the overseas department
named John Ward. (He later moved on to run the union for senior civil
servants, with the catchy title First Division Association.) By 1979
morale was sapped by the Bank's determination throughout 1975 and
1976 to conform exactly to the government's incomes policy. Gordon
Richardson himself waived £6,000 due from a wage increase in 1979,
when he was paid £51,980, and most senior economists at the Bank
still regarded incomes policy as the answer to a Keynesian's prayer.
This added another dimension to Ward's problem. 'Richardson was
surrounded by people who are highly motivated by fascinating jobs. It
is difficult for him to know what morale is like on the shop floor, but
there are senior people just below that level who believe they were sold
a false prospectus by the Bank,' he said. Some of the senior men
boycotted the Governor's cricket match in 1975, and by 1979 wage
levels had fallen perceptibly below those of the clearers. BESO was
actually threatening to ballot the staff on industrial action unless the
Governor managed to improve matters. (He did.) The objectives of
BESO may sound modest, but within the Bank they bordered on
mutiny. 'One doesn't hoist the Red Flag and get rid of all the managers.
It's more basic than that. It's about the boy and girl in the office being
able to talk freely to their managers about the way they work,' said
Ward.

Changes had certainly occurred in the 1970s – it was no longer a
rule that junior employees did not speak until they were spoken to –
but the Bank was still a hierarchical and authoritarian place.
Richardson preferred to be called 'Mr Governor' by all but his most

senior officials. (Imagine, therefore, the agitation caused by a young woman called Shamla Katka from the registrar's department who posed for *Mayfair* magazine under the headline 'The Naughty Young Lady of Threadneedle Street'.) Decisions were taken by small groups of people who rarely felt the need to explain them. Individuality was not admired.

Choosing one adjective to describe the Bank, Kit McMahon had offered 'stylish': this was no doubt true of his own activities, but many of the staff would have suggested 'stuffy'. In the late 1970s the personnel department became aware that a number of able employees with marketable skills, like foreign-exchange dealers and economists, were quitting to join the City's private sector. And then, late in 1979, another involuntary change took place that was to affect the Bank profoundly.

Before 1979 the Hollom/Blunden efficiency drive had only a marginal effect on the number of full-time employees at the Bank. They numbered 7,000 in 1970; 6,975 in 1975, and just over 6,800 in 1979. Then in the next two years they fell sharply to just under 5,600, or by 18 per cent. (Aggregate pay, however, rose from £37.4 million to £50.7 million during the same two-year period, suggesting that the Governor did indeed improve matters as far as pay was concerned; certainly all talk about industrial action stopped.) The drop in staff numbers was begun by computerization, but the bulk of it was caused by the end of exchange control.

In opposition the Conservative Party had promised the progressive dismantling of exchange controls, but no one in the Bank expected the new government to be as progressive as it proved to be after its victory in May 1979. The Bank had thought in terms of two years, but the whole exchange-control apparatus was completely demolished by 23 October 1979. An autumn weekend left 675 employees without work to do. For some it meant that there was no longer any use at all for the special skills they had developed over decades.

The exchange-control department had been monitoring the export of money from Britain for forty years. Leslie O'Brien made his reputation as an exchange controller at the beginning of the war, and the Bank had accumulated expertise in the most arcane varieties of trade. There were few things it did not know about the intricacies of markets for stamps, or diamonds, or commodities. The last departmental head was Douglas Dawkins, who observes: 'Exchange control gave the Bank a wider window on the world than it has ever had.'

The powers delegated to the Bank by the Exchange Control Act were as comprehensive as could be: no individual or company could transfer any substantial sum of money abroad without the permission of the Bank. The power was absolute. (The Bank had power to contradict its own notices: having made the rules, it was allowed to break them.) Dawkins says: 'You could give responsibility to people who were relatively young, which was unusual in the Bank. They met senior people from outside; they made real decisions and they had to stand by them – immensely important in developing younger staff.'

Exchange control was a manifestation of the Bank's authority, and as time went by the department's own attitudes revealed a shift in the basis of that authority. Dawkins observes: 'The Act worked because it was a statutory requirement and because it was implemented by the Bank via its moral authority. Originally, we relied on authority, and we were at pains to be fair, to avoid arbitrary and capricious decisions; we had a reputation for open-mindedness and common sense. But as time went by and overseas institutions were less inclined to accept the Bank's moral authority, it became more necessary to rely on the statute. The Bank's authority is a curious and a subtle thing: you can use it only when you are sure it's going to work.' This was more evidence of the trend outside the Bank towards rule-making. It was just like the Banking Bill. Authority was take over statutory rather than moral.

There were incidental implications for the Bank's authority in the City when the exchange-control department suddenly closed down. Residual control over the London Metal Exchange had to be wound up also. The Bank had had no supervisory responsibility for commodity trading, but was able to threaten to use its exchange-control powers to deter organizations like the LME from deviating from the Bank's norms of behaviour. Those deterrent powers were based, quite simply, on fear: businessmen depended on the goodwill of the Bank to allow them to finance their international trade. When there was no longer any need to fear the Bank, its authority would necessarily be diminished. Nothing seems so hollow as a prefect's authority once children have left school, and there is a tendency to retrospective derision. It is easy to overstate this case, but unwise to ignore it. After the end of exchange control, the Bank's power depended more on its moral authority. It was even more important than before that the Bank should not make mistakes.

As for the exchange controllers, some found it difficult to adjust to new work, but 400 of the 675 stayed on. 'People accustomed to making decisions are generally welcomed,' says Dawkins. (Though some of the sparky intellectuals in Threadneedle Street regarded colleagues from exchange control as the sort of dullards who made the Bank more stodgy and less efficient.)

To help absorb redundant exchange controllers, and smooth the process of computerization, the Bank introduced a voluntary redundancy scheme. A remarkable number of people seemed anxious to leave, and 730 applications were accepted – more than 10 per cent of the staff. Inside the Bank 600 employees were transferred to new jobs. There were no compulsory redundancies, but it was still a nerve-racking business, and on 16 January 1980 this uncertainty spread to the most senior levels of the staff when Gordon Richardson announced a fundamental reorganization of the power structure. This had little to do with the end of exchange control, however. True to his nature, Richardson had been mulling over these changes for five years – he had first asked Blunden for his opinion about them in 1975. But they were no less dramatic for having taken so long to gestate, for Richardson did nothing less than demolish the traditional source of executive power in the Bank – the chief cashier's office. It was replaced by a new executive élite which would be more responsive to the wishes of the Governor.

The chief cashier's office was on the ground floor of Threadneedle Street, its name carved in gilded capital letters above an imposing doorway, and the chief cashier himself sat in one of the desirable suites overlooking Garden Court. It was the department that all bright young men hoped to join. David Somerset, deputy chief cashier in the 1970s, says: 'Chief cashier's was where all the interesting new jobs went. They had all the best people, and you didn't do well in the Bank unless you'd done well there.' The department dealt directly with the domestic money market, and acted on the government's behalf in the gilt market. It was the area in which the Bank behaved most like a bank.

The post of chief cashier was encrusted with tradition. Abraham Newland, of whom there are more portraits in the Bank than of any other single figure (one is by Zoffany), was a legendary figure in the eighteenth century. What was striking about the elevation of Leslie

O'Brien was that he was the first chief cashier to become Governor, for the roles were quite distinct. True, the chief cashier might have his name on the banknotes, but public pronouncements from the Bank were made by the Governor. The chief cashier was chief executive, and expected to perform his duties discreetly in the background.

The Bank's organization chart showed the Governor at the top, with the deputy governor and a small cluster of executive directors with particular interests but no specific responsibilities directly underneath him. Below them on the chart came the departmental heads, who went about the Bank's daily business. They reported to the chief cashier, who, although a departmental head himself, was first among equals and reported only to the Governor. To emphasize his status, no memorandum went to the Governor without having been initialled by the chief cashier, and any letter containing a statement of Bank policy had to be signed by him. Indeed, any member of the staff who wanted to talk to someone outside the Bank was supposed to get the chief cashier's permission beforehand. The theory, as stated by one senior member of the department in the 1970s, was: 'You can't have economists rushing out and shooting their mouths off.'

It was a system of management that worked only in a hierarchical organization, and it was a great source of irritation to the distinguished figures who were imported by the Governor from posts outside the Bank to become executive directors. At the beginning of 1980 two (McMahon and Fforde) had come from Oxford, and one (Dow) from the civil service and O E C D. They were all economists, and the chief cashier, John Page, was deeply sceptical about economists. In his vocabulary, 'economist' was a dirty word. Before long, two of the dirty words in Christopher Dow's vocabulary were 'chief cashier'.

Dow's indignation was fuelled by an episode in which, as one of the Governor's leading economic advisers, he asked the head of the economic-intelligence department to do a job for him. 'He was a terribly nice chap, but very stubborn, and he said he couldn't do it,' Dow says. Apparently, the request had come through the wrong channel, and could be properly made only by the chief cashier. Dow was outraged. 'I felt I had to shout in order to get people to do things,' he says. The noise eventually came to Page's attention. He approached Dow. 'You don't want his head, do you?' he asked. Dow said he did not want the chief of the economic-intelligence department sacked; the relationship remained edgy.

Richardson was determined to alter the balance of power, but wished to achieve this by means of a legitimate management reorganization rather than a punitive raid on a traditional barony. The means he used was an inquiry, which he asked Sir Douglas Allen to undertake. Allen, who had retired from the Treasury (where he had been permanent secretary), was now Lord Croham, and had been lured by Richardson to join the Bank as a special adviser. There were few more distinguished figures in British public life, but to any old Bank man, Allen's inquiry was not good news. It was like appointing an Australian to propose the reorganization of English cricket: he might get it right but his motives would always be suspect.

On his arrival in Threadneedle Street, Allen suffered from culture shock: 'The organization of the Bank was not what we in the Treasury thought it was.' Specifically, there were four senior men with the title executive director who had no executive power. To discover how this curiosity arose Allen adopted the historical method, beginning, as all diligent inquirers into the Bank of England should, with Walter Bagehot's *Lombard Street*, published in 1873. In those days, Bagehot thought the chief cashier was like the permanent secretary of the Foreign or Home Offices, and declared the system perfectly sound since it relieved the Governor of onerous administrative tasks. 'Banking ought never to be an exceedingly laborious trade,' wrote Bagehot. 'There must be great want of system and a great deficiency of skilled assistance if extreme labour is thrown upon the chief.'

Montagu Norman's view was quite the reverse. He was the second Governor to serve more than the traditional two-year term (his lasted twenty-six years) and the first to reinforce his position with executive directors who had seats on the Court. The other directors on the Court were suspicious, fearing domination by the new, full-time men, and the limit of four they imposed on the number of paid executives the Governor could hire was incorporated in the Bank of England Act, 1946. This was the source of Richardson's frustration, and Allen's solution.

Allen concluded that the Governor could appoint as many directors as he liked just as long as no more than four were on the Court. Call them associate directors, or assistant directors, and they will be perfectly legal, he said. Next Allen recommended that the Bank's directors — executive or associate — be given executive responsibilities. The associate directors did not actually need a seat on

109

the Court to be able to report to it. Anyway, Allen said, the role of the Court was so much reduced that this detail hardly mattered. These conclusions suited the Governor's purpose admirably. Allen observed: 'Richardson wanted to increase the exposure of the policy side of the Bank. His main interest was policy, not organization. He felt, I deduced, that the organization could look after itself.' Richardson had also decided whom he intended to promote.

This coincided with the retirement of the deputy governor, Sir Jasper Hollom, and was outlined in a message to the staff. 'You will not be surprised to learn,' it said, 'that after the economic and financial convulsions of the last decade, the extension of the Bank's supervisory functions, and the abolition of exchange control, some further changes in the management structure have in my opinion become desirable.' The message was that the people concerned with domestic and external monetary policy would be grouped more closely in a policy and markets division. Banking supervision and surveillance of the City's securities and commodities markets would make up a second division. A third would be called the operations and services division: this would contain everything that was not included in the first two. The old departmental structure had been dissolved at a stroke. Richardson could not have proceeded with so radical a move had he not had the support of the existing executive directors – Kit McMahon, who became deputy governor, John Fforde, Christopher Dow and George Blunden, who claimed that he had outlined the framework of the reorganization five years earlier, when he was first asked about it. He took over the operations and services division ('virtually a second deputy governor,' noted Allen). Richardson needed their support in view of an explosive sentence in the middle of his message: 'The chief cashier will in future be responsible only for banking work and will no longer be concerned with monetary policy and its execution, and will cease to exercise administrative responsibilities ranging more widely over the Bank as a whole.' A tradition that had lasted for 286 years was shattered in forty words.

John Page received some compensation: he moved into the executive directorship made vacant by McMahon's promotion and was put in charge of the banking-supervision division, where he lingered for a year or two before leaving the Bank for good. Having been outmanoeuvred, Page did not contest the reorganization – not that he thought it was a good thing, just that he felt it was what a majority of people in the Bank wanted. His colleagues from the old chief cashier's department were not so philosophical. His successor, David Somerset, was titled Chief of the Banking Department, a second-rank job in Blunden's division. (An appendix to the Governor's message noted that Somerset would 'bear the traditional title chief cashier for statutory reasons'.) On hearing details, a small group from the new banking department immediately went to Blunden to express the distress they felt, distress which did not grow less with the passage of time. Here is a random selection of their judgements five years later:

> Gordon Richardson's objective was to create a shadow civil-service institution.
> Richardson was bored with the problems of departments like registrar's. They didn't fire his imagination.
> I don't think Gordon Richardson was aware that there was a banking department.
> Gordon Richardson was bored with banking.
> The reorganization was a cock-up.

The Bank had been formally partitioned. In the divisions there was a staff of 450 that formed a clear élite, led by executive directors and younger associate and assistant directors whom Richardson had been anxious to promote – Eddie George in the money-markets division, David Walker in finance and industry, and Anthony Loehnis in the overseas department. The remainder worked in the unfashionable operational areas of the Bank. Moreover, the banking and registrar's departments and the printing works were expected to bear the burden of the further manpower cuts that became necessary when the Treasury imposed its cash-limits policy on public bodies in 1980. By February 1983 the full-time staff had fallen to 5,200 – 24 per cent down on the 1970 figure. Elsewhere, ceilings were placed on expansion plans within the divisions. Bank supervision was allocated no more than seventy-five men and women to apply the Banking Act, 1979. Although the tasks were not comparable, it is an indication of the new and old Banks that this was exactly one tenth of the manpower deployed to operate the Exchange Control Act.

The drop in numbers employed was announced as a matter of pride in the 1985 *Annual Report*. But the enthusiasm was not universally shared within the Bank. David Somerset was concerned for the efficiency of the Bank following such deep cuts in the staff: 'In the old days we went to great lengths to see that we didn't make mistakes. We were enormously overmanned, but we made fewer mistakes. By the 1980s we were doing more things with fewer people, and we began to make more mistakes than we used to.'

Richardson had successfully moulded an image for the Bank of effortless superiority. By the early 1980s, it needed a lot more effort to appear superior.

7

Humbling the Great Panjandrum

One of the executive directors vividly recalls Gordon Richardson's mood when he returned from his first meeting with Margaret Thatcher after she became Prime Minister. He was glowing with pleasure at the application of a new broom to economic policy. People would be surprised, he told his colleagues, at how different a Thatcher government was going to be.

Richardson's sense of anticipation was founded on the belief that he shared the broad economic objectives of the government, and most of all its determination to bring the rate of inflation under control. When Mrs Thatcher came to power Richardson had almost four years of his second term to serve and he was indeed to be surprised at how different this period would be. Alas, the Prime Minister and the Governor proved to be incompatible. 'It was like the difference between cat people and dog people,' says one observer who had to sit in the room with them.

To understand the degree of disenchantment that soon set in, it will help if we review the various forms of relationship between governments and central banks. There is the uncomplicated relationship: the central bank is either completely independent or completely dependent, one or the other. The Bundesbank and the Federal Reserve Board are examples of independent central banks (although the Federal Reserve's freedom to intervene in foreign-exchange markets is curbed by the US Treasury). The Banque de France is a case of the dependent. The Bank of England has always claimed that the quality of its advice to Whitehall and its authority in the City give a form of independence, despite the limitations of the Bank of England Act. There was evidence of this *de facto* independence at the beginning and the end of the 1970s, but, as we have seen, in that brief period the degree of independence of the Bank was subject to ebbs and flows.

While in opposition, the Conservatives began in 1977 to fill in the details of their economic policy, and it contained a remarkably enticing prospect for the Bank. These were the heroic days of Thatcherism in which economic policy was to be guided by the free forces of the market and not by government. Following the logic of that argument, the implications for the Bank were considerable. One of the authors of the Conservative policy was David Howell, who became Energy Minister in the first Thatcher Cabinet, and in his book *Blind Victory* he outlines the concept that developed in Opposition:

There was strong sympathy for the idea that monetary policy, although not the be-all and end-all, was too important and complex to be left in the centre of the political arena, and that we could do worse than follow the German example of placing monetary judgements in more independent hands. In other words, if the Bank of England could be given the independence from the politicians of, for example, the German Bundesbank, the management of monetary policy could be taken out of the front line, overselling of monetarism avoided, and government policy generally presented in less abstract and desiccated form.

This was the freedom the Bank had always envied in the German and American central banks. The prospect should have sent waves of anticipation flowing down Threadneedle Street, but when Howell asked friends at the Bank what they thought of the idea he was told that it would never happen. Douglas Allen would have said the same thing if Howell had asked him: 'There is an inherent refusal in politicians to say that monetary policy is not their affair,' Howell had made a second misjudgement about the future Prime Minister. She was not in the least afraid of overselling monetarism. Quite the contrary.

When the Conservatives came to power they were happy to be identified with monetarism. Mrs Thatcher's adoption of the M3 money target was an affirmation of belief. For the Bank, M3 had been rather more of a political convenience, designed to draw the attention of politicians to inflation. So here, from the start, was potential conflict between believing and unbelieving monetarists, and while a number of old Keynesians in the Treasury may have appreciated the Bank's delicate neo-monetarist stance, they were being weeded out by the Thatcherites. The Treasury soon began to sound notably more doctrinaire. This was not because the Chancellor, Sir Geoffrey Howe, was a dogmatist. He was nothing of the kind. But Nigel Lawson, the Financial Secretary, was a zealous Thatcherite, and the Prime Minister herself showed no desire to leave economic policy to the Chancellor.

The trouble was that M3 consistently failed to behave in the way the Conservatives expected it to. Within a few months of the election M3 was rising faster than forecast, and the Treasury dealt firmly with this by increasing interest rates. The price of controlling M3 was a 17 per cent minimum lending rate, and the impact of this unprecedented rate soon spread to other economic indices. Sterling became an extremely profitable short-term investment for foreign banks and speculators, who bought pounds. Up shot the exchange rate; down came exports, and this exacerbated the rise in unemployment. Profits fell too, curbing new investment. And still inflation did not go away.

This evidence of economic crisis actually served to strengthen the government's belief in M3 – the sum of deposits by British residents and companies in British banks. In the Medium-term Financial Strategy, published by the Treasury in March 1980, targets for M3 were established for years ahead, beginning with a rise in the range of 7–11 per cent in 1980–81. But there was a further problem associated with M3, and this was caused by another of the government's new economic policies. When exchange controls ended in October 1979, one of the compelling reasons for British residents and companies to deposit their money with British banks was removed. Since the banks were also operating the credit-control system known as 'the corset', they were at a competitive disadvantage with financial institutions outside the banking system, at home and abroad. These two factors caused money to move out of British banks, often into offshore accounts. (In banking jargon, this is *disintermediation*.) These movements distorted M3, and the Bank's technical explanation strengthened the argument that a true notion of M3 would be available only after the removal of 'the corset'. This was done in the summer of 1980, and the British banks celebrated their independence by going on a lending spree. So anxious were the banks to lend that they offered mortgages for the first time, and the consequence was that a great deal of the money that had moved out of the British banking system moved back into it. (*Reintermediation*, in the jargon.) The effect on the monetary target was instantaneous. M3 spiralled wildly out of control. The Prime Minister went wild too. It was time, she declared, to bring the Bank to heel. Given the choice between dependence and independence, the notions that had attracted Howell before the election were rejected out of hand. The Prime Minister wanted the Bank to be more, not less, dependent on government, and there was no better way to start the process, she thought, than by appointing a new Governor.

This was more easily said than done. The same idea had occurred to Sir Geoffrey Howe, but he discovered that he had no power to sack Richardson. He reported this to the Prime Minister, who was not daunted: 'It says on the plate on my front door that I'm the First Lord of the Treasury, so Richardson must do what I say,' she told the Chancellor. But she was stuck with her Governor until 1983, and all she could do was order him to come to Downing Street with his senior men and explain how this unforeseen disaster to M3 had occurred. The usual explanations were rehearsed: the markets were agitated, the effects of disintermediation and reintermediation had been more volatile than the Bank or the Treasury, for that matter, had forecast. If everyone remained cool, the Governor said, M3 would adjust before long and fall to within range of the target. That was the Bank's script, but the Prime Minister was not listening. She watched M3 rise by 19 per cent – almost as much as in 1973, when her great antagonist Edward Heath was Prime Minister – and she made up her mind about the Bank. Either it was technically incompetent (it could not achieve the monetary target), or it was subversive (it was undermining monetarism). Though these were contradictory accusations, in the autumn of 1980 Mrs Thatcher appeared to believe both. The time had come, she decided, for the Governor of the Bank of England to be taught a lesson or two by some of her friends who also knew about economics. Richardson sulked.

The Prime Minister enjoyed argument, and she respected people who took her on. The Governor, on the other hand, was not accustomed to rough and tumble. He preferred to establish a consensus in which, ideally, the last word was his. For some time now, when he descended on Whitehall, Richardson had been able to debate on terms dictated by him, as Leon Brittan, who was chief secretary to the Treasury in the new Tory government, confirms: 'The Treasury were still a little wary of the Bank, and the Governor was very powerful. Geoffrey Howe was reluctant to take him on and was embarrassed by the conflict with Number Ten.'

Although the customary formalities were still observed, behind the scenes in Whitehall and Threadneedle Street the language was rancorous:

> Gordon Richardson was like a grand panjandrum. His own officials, including Kit McMahon, were loath to disagree with him in his presence. He looked fastidious and spoke with what was meant to be authority; there was no intellectual dialogue to be had with him. (Treasury minister)

> The Prime Minister found Gordon Richardson a pain. He is not a character one can warm to and her view was that he required fairly precise instructions. (Downing Street adviser)

> She felt he lectured her. (Senior Bank official)

117

Richardson was never willing to flirt with the Prime Minister or to charm her in any way. We knew this was the way to get along with her, but he couldn't do it. (Senior Bank official)

The Governor himself felt that the Thatcherites' accusation that the removal of 'the corset' was designed to undermine the government was unpardonable. One of his colleagues notes:

Gordon Richardson was most hurt when his motives were challenged, and what really wounded him was the charge that the Bank had been dishonourable. The charge implied that the Bank had been unprofessional, and this weakened the position of the Bank quite unjustly.

The personal falling-out between the Prime Minister and the Governor was reflected in the relationship between the Bank and the Treasury, and the man most grieved by this was Richardson, whose sympathy for the government's broad objectives made him a natural ally. Once he felt secure at the Bank by 1977, his ambitions both for himself and the institution had continued to grow, and had certainly not been satisfied by 1980. One close colleague reports that the Governor felt that he could have been to the field of monetary policy what Lord Carrington, the Foreign Secretary, was to foreign policy. Instead he was drawn into a lively and sometimes bad-tempered contest which concerned, among other things, the Bank's reputation for technical competence.

Questions about technical competence were posed by the Treasury at the very beginning of the contest. Nigel Lawson had sufficient knowledge of the techniques of monetary management to be able to needle Richardson with sharp observations about the Bank's reading of the markets. Lawson had always been politically ambitious, and had written speeches for Sir Alec Douglas-Home in 1964, but while he waited for a parliamentary seat to materialize he had worked as a journalist. He started on the *Financial Times*, and was the first editor of the *Sunday Telegraph* City section, setting a style for brief, well-informed and opinionated comment which survived his departure. As editor of the *Spectator*, his generous private behaviour suggested that his public strut and bluster might be a front. But when he became an MP, what the Commons saw was the bluster. He was one of Mrs Thatcher's barkers, shouting at the Opposition, and while it won him few friends, it did influence the Party leader. He was the only one of

118

the barkers to be given a proper job after the 1979 election. Lawson was the cleverest of them, and he shared with his leader (and with a number of journalists) a suspicion of the *ex cathedra* pronouncements of establishment grandees like the Governor of the Bank of England. Now that he was Financial Secretary of the Treasury he could do something about it.

What he did, just occasionally, was to question the Bank's judgement about the state of the market. Indeed, Lawson argued about precise details of a securities issue with the Bank's experts. They were led by Eddie George, now assistant director in the money-markets division, and he was disinclined to be told by a junior minister whether an issue should, in the jargon, be £40 or £30 paid. Of course, George accepted that the ultimate responsibility was the Treasury's but when officials, encouraged by Lawson, started to interfere, George insisted that their advice should be channelled through the Chancellor. After further consultation, George's view usually prevailed, but the Bank was conscious that the Treasury was relishing the opportunity to take revenge for the period of the Bank's 'effortless superiority'. This phase of the contest came to an end only when Lawson actually informed the Bank what year a particular loan issue should be redeemed. George proposed an issue of, say, $13\frac{1}{2}$ per cent Treasury stock 1994, and was informed that it ought to be redeemed in 1995 instead. The Bank began the fight back. The Treasury was informed that no government securities would be issued until the difference was resolved. George stated that since issuing securities was not necessarily a Bank monopoly, the Treasury could do it if the Chancellor chose, but the operation required technical consistency; the Bank could not act on arbitrary loan instructions. If civil servants wanted to make policy for one loan issue, they must be willing to follow through and take responsibility for the whole process. At this point the Chancellor demurred: 'When push came to shove, the Treasury declined the responsibility,' says a colleague of George's.

These incidents revived the Bank's confidence a little. The government had been persuaded, albeit reluctantly, that the Bank was not without technical expertise in the markets. But the debate about monetarism was unresolved. The monetarists outside the government were still insisting that the Bank's practical monetarism was a sham; some argued that interest rates should rise even higher. Mrs Thatcher was not certain, and she called in reinforcements, led by one of Britain's leading academic monetarists, Alan Walters. In January 1981 he was brought back from 'exile' in the United States, and installed in the Cabinet Office.

On his arrival in Whitehall, Walters remembers, he found the Bank at daggers drawn with Whitehall: 'alienated and sounding off'. He discovered, he says, that if he pursued an argument with the Bank, they would tend to stonewall him with technical devices. Mrs Thatcher decided that it was time the Governor and his colleagues were quite literally taught a lesson, and, since she was interested, she would learn with them. Richardson and his advisers were invited to Downing Street, given tea, and lectured on the virtues of monetarism by reputable American economists like Karl Brunner and Allan Meltzer. The President of the Swiss central bank, Fritz Leutwiler, was called in to discuss exchange-rate policy.

Mrs Thatcher listened carefully. From Brunner and Meltzer she learned that real monetarists did not consider the British government's monetary targets to be monetarist at all. Both favoured a system called monetary-base control, in which interest rates are allowed to adjust automatically to changes in a selected monetary target. For monetarists, the virtue of the system is that it reduces the power of the government or, indeed, the central bank, to interfere in the market mechanism for pricing money. The case against it is a side-effect – wild swings in interest rates. The Bank's attack on monetary-base control was concentrated on that point, for a modified version of the system had pushed American interest rates over 20 per cent earlier in 1980. The Bank said its studies showed that in Britain the volatility inherent in the system would be 'unacceptable'.

Walters watched the Prime Minister. 'She'd rush in with the argument, but she was cautious about reform.' She understood that interest rates could rise above 20 per cent before the new system settled in, and that made her anxious. She recalled the impact on house-buyers with mortgages ('our own people') when interest rates had risen to 17 per cent in 1979 and 1980. Moreover, higher interest rates, with their depressing impact on industry, would certainly not reduce unemployment. Having listened carefully to the case for and against monetary-base control Mrs Thatcher proved to be less of a theorist than her admirers thought, and the concept was quietly forgotten. The battle for rigorous monetarism having been lost by the monetarists, the charges that the Bank was conspiring against the government were dropped also. 'Once we'd persuaded the government we weren't trying to do them down, it became much more relaxed,' says one participant. Coincidentally, the M3 target was by then being met and inflation was falling. The Prime Minister looked at the figures and concluded that since her policy was working, the Bank must be doing something right at last.

Though the Prime Minister grew no fonder of Gordon Richardson, the relationship between the Chancellor and the Governor became less strained, though the two were rarely on the same wavelength. Meetings between the Treasury and the Bank tended to sound like scenes from 'Yes, Minister'. One participant recalls a dialogue:

CHANCELLOR: Would you like to start?
GOVERNOR: No, you start.
CHANCELLOR: I think we're rather agnostic about this.
PERMANENT SECRETARY: We're not agnostic at all. Surely, Chancellor, we had agreed this would be done?
GOVERNOR: Well, we're opposed. I think we all are. What do you think, Mr George?
GEORGE: Yes, Governor.

On hearing the Governor's latest proposals, Howe would sometimes fall completely silent, and Richardson would assume that silence meant consent. When this was not the case, senior officials from the Bank and the civil service would have to cobble together a form of agreement, and they soon discovered that they were rather good at doing so. A new permanent secretary named Peter Middleton, a favourite of the Prime Minister, had taken over from Sir Douglas Wass at the Treasury, and Alan Walters had settled comfortably at the Cabinet Office. When Walters became better acquainted with Eddie George, he discovered much common ground: 'Eddie wanted to keep inflation down. I got on very well with Eddie,' says Walters.

Since Walters had his own strong ideas about techniques of funding government debt, which was George's own speciality, they did not always agree. Walters, for instance, favoured index-linked securities, an idea which the Bank did not immediately warm to. The Governor was especially offended by index-linked bonds, which he associated with banana republics, but the Prime Minister liked the scheme, and when they were introduced the Bank had to admit they were very popular. Walters would sort out various disagreements with George; Peter Middleton and George would smooth away mis-understandings between the Governor and the Chancellor. In fact they formed a powerful troika, perhaps more influential than their chiefs realized (especially on exchange-rate policy), which is why officials who remain in Whitehall and at the Bank are reluctant to admit it. But Alan Walters, having returned to Washington DC, has no such inhibitions. His description of the operation of monetary policy after 1981 goes like this: 'When anything needed to be decided, I brought the Prime Minister along. Peter Middleton brought the Chancellor along, and Eddie George brought the Governor along.' Most of the time it worked like a charm: Mrs Thatcher was appeased and the Treasury stopped sniping at the Bank, for the time being at least. In Threadneedle Street, confidence was slowly being restored.

By the spring of 1981 the Governor's attention had been attrac-ted by another matter, which later came to obsess him and cause him to exert all the authority he could muster. It began when Standard Chartered did the proper thing and informed the Bank of England that it proposed to bid for the Royal Bank of Scotland Group. This merger made sound sense. Standard Chartered's business was overseas mostly, in the Far East, Africa and the United States. It lacked a solid English base, and since the Royal Group included the English branches of Williams and Glyns Bank, the merger would transform Standard Chartered into the fifth English clearing bank. The Governor let it be known that he was perfectly happy with the proposed merger, and the directors of both banks thought that was all the preparation necessary. Standard Chartered did not even take the precaution of buying Royal Bank shares on the market before 17 March 1981, when they announced a bid which valued the Royal Bank at £334 million.

Then Michael Sandberg made his appearance in Threadneedle Street. Sandberg was chairman of the Hongkong and Shanghai Banking Corporation, known to the English in the Far East as the. Honkers and Shankers. It was Standard Chartered's great rival in the East, where it had been out-performing the London-based bank for some years. Adventurous as the Hong Kong entrepreneurs it financed, it had already established a substantial base in New York, buying the Marine Midland Bank there. In Hong Kong, where a piratical style of business is taken for granted, Sandberg cut a substantial figure. The Governor in London, however, declined to be impressed. Sandberg sought an audience with Richardson to tell him that he proposed making a counter-bid for the Royal Bank, which he hoped to transform into the Hongkong and Shanghai's 'flagship in Europe'. Moreover, he named a price much higher than Standard Chartered had even thought of.

Richardson pondered only briefly before telling Sandberg that his bid would not have the Bank's approval. Despite this rejection, Sandberg agreed to consult the Bank about any further plans he might have. The next day, 6 April, the Hongkong and Shanghai Bank announced a bid of £498 million for the Royal Bank. Since the Bank of England had to learn of this from the news agencies, it was interpreted as an act of *lèse-majesté*. The reaction was indignant; now the Bank 'strongly disapproved' of Sandberg's bid. Standard Chartered raised its bid on 23 April to £480 million, which, with the Royal Bank's share value wobbling up and down on the market, was worth £10 million more than the Hongkong and Shanghai offer. The bidding stopped there, for on 1 May both proposals were referred to the Monopolies Commission.

The Bank's case against the merger between the Royal Bank and the Hongkong and Shanghai Bank to the Monopolies Commission was extraordinary. Every weapon in its armoury was discharged, including one that seemed to be entirely against the tenor of the times. While foreign banks were setting up branches in London as fast as factories were closing down, Richardson's basic case was that a foreign bank could not be trusted to own a clearing bank, especially the Hongkong and Shanghai. The reason given to begin with was just that the bank was foreign. A foreign bank, said the Bank to the Commission, would be less sensitive to broad economic issues in the UK and so could not be relied upon to help in maintaining the stability of the British financial system in time of crisis. Nor could foreigners be relied on to finance local industry, like North Sea oil, or to prop up failing companies.

Next the Bank drew attention to conflicts of interest that might arise between the parent bank's country and the government of the UK. It was not easy to grasp immediately the direct relevance of this argument, since Hong Kong is a crown colony, but this was a subtle pointer to the Chinese card. What it meant was that after 1997 the Hongkong and Shanghai Bank might be in thrall to unpredictable politicians in Beijing.

123

Then there was the problem of prudential supervision. The Basle agreement between supervisors stated that ultimate responsibility for supervision rested with the parent authority – the Hong Kong administration, if the bid were accepted. Since the Hongkong and Shanghai was so powerful in Hong Kong 'this would cause the supervisory authorities great difficulties if their requirements should run contrary to the Hongkong and Shanghai Bank's'. In other words, the bank effectively ran the colony's banking community and the British administration of Hong Kong could not be trusted to see fair play. The Hong Kong government sent a senior official to London to explain that the banking rules were being changed, and that American bank supervisors had been perfectly satisfied when the Marine Midland of New York was taken over by the Hong Kong bank. Not good enough, replied the Bank of England, where the reputation of the New York State banking commissioners was not high.

As the case developed, it became clear that the real problem was Sandberg's lack of respect for the Bank. The implications of this were momentous for the Bank, and they were spelled out in the Monopolies Commission report on the reference, as follows: The fact that the Hongkong and Shanghai Banking Corporation (HSBC)

> was prepared to go ahead with the bid in the face of opposition from the Governor of the Bank suggested that the HSBC would not always be prepared to accept the Bank's customary authority and therefore would not necessarily provide the kind of cooperation the Bank expected from clearing banks. Moreover, if the HSBC was allowed to go ahead this would make it more difficult for the Bank to exercise its customary authority ... If the Bank's authority was not fully accepted by the clearing banks, other more dirigiste, less flexible, and in the Bank's view less effective methods of dealing with the banking community would have to be introduced and the existing, well-tried and well-respected system would be compromised.

A symptom of Richardson's obsession was his unwillingness to trust the Commission to reach the right conclusion. While its investigation was under way, Richardson conceived an extraordinary scheme. He decided the way to solve the problem once and for all would be for Parliament to pass a one-paragraph amendment to the Banking Act 1979 giving the Bank of England reserve powers to block selected takeovers of British banks by foreigners – especially if they were called Sandberg and came from Hong Kong.

First reactions in the Treasury were sceptical. How, civil servants asked ministers, would the British government react if the California legislature ruled that the Midland Bank could not buy the Crocker National Bank of San Francisco? (The Midland was in the process of doing so; if California had legislated to prevent the purchase it would, as it turned out, have saved the Midland a great deal of money and humiliation.) It was a reflection of Richardson's authority that despite the Treasury's misgivings, the Chancellor submitted a paper to the Cabinet's economic strategy committee outlining the Governor's proposals. It was also an indication of the limits of his authority, because the idea was brutally squashed by the Foreign Office and the Department of Trade and Industry. The strength of the Bank's feeling had already disturbed these departments. The Foreign Office took a jaundiced view of the Bank's criticism of the capability of the Hong Kong administration; it was run by their men, after all, and the resentment felt in Hong Kong was voiced in London by the diplomatic service. The Department of Trade and Industry was worried about retaliation: they feared a large industrial order might be lost.

Towards the end of 1981 there was speculation in Whitehall that if Richardson did not have his way he would consider threatening to use his ultimate deterrent – resignation. Normally this would provoke grave disquiet in the Treasury, for it was a common assumption that the resignation of the Governor of the Bank of England would result in appalling turmoil in the markets. Sandberg heard the rumours from allies in Whitehall and told cronies that the government was sufficiently disaffected for the resignation to be accepted. A senior Treasury man remarked: 'If he again says "over my dead body" then she might say "thank you" and bury him.' But the debate became academic with the publication of the Monopolies Commission report. In January 1982 it announced that 'either merger may be expected to operate against the public interest'. True, two of the four commissioners saw no reason why Standard Chartered's bid should be prevented, but a majority was needed to allow the bid to go ahead. The commissioners had not swallowed the Bank's arguments whole – they were more confident of the abilities of Hong Kong supervisors, for instance – but the majority had been persuaded that the effects on career prospects, initiative and business enterprise in Scotland would be damaged if the

Royal Bank of Scotland were taken over. In retrospect it sounds less convincing, but it was entirely acceptable in Threadneedle Street at the time.

Although Richardson's term had another year to run, and he was to experience further triumphs, these took place abroad. In London the fight against the Hongkong and Shanghai Banking Corporation began to look like a last hurrah. When central bankers and finance ministers met in Toronto for the annual meeting of the World Bank and the International Monetary Fund in the autumn of 1982, there was already eager speculation about his succession. (At the meeting the Mexican government precipitated the world debt crisis, and Richardson's commanding role in grappling with it is the main subject of the next chapter.) That September the list of potential successors was being circulated. A predictable name was Sir Jeremy Morse, the chairman of Lloyds Bank, who had been a director of the Bank before taking the chairmanship of an IMF committee that had tried bravely to establish an orderly international monetary system after the collapse of the Bretton Woods mechanism in the early 1970s. That failed, but the breadth of Sir Jeremy's experience made him a safe choice for the list, except that he had been critical of the Government's passion for monetarism, and its raid on the clearer's 'windfall profits' in 1981. The name of David Scholey of S. G. Warburg was always to be found on lists like this, but, as a candidate, while he always made it to the starting line, he did not really run. To many central bankers, especially from abroad, the obvious candidate was Kit McMahon, who had undergone a long and distinguished apprenticeship at the Bank and had many admirers in the Treasury. There were two obstacles in his case: a certain *froideur* had developed in his relationship with Richardson after the break-up of McMahon's marriage, and the Governor did not push his name in Whitehall; and in the Treasury, there was grave doubt whether Mrs Thatcher would accept a candidate whom she associated with the troubled first act of her premiership.

The surprise contender was Philip Haddon Cave, the financial secretary of the Hong Kong administration. The chief secretary of the Treasury, Leon Brittan, thought Haddon Cave would be a breath of fresh air in Threadneedle Street. So did his brother Samuel Brittan, who writes an influential weekly column in the *Financial Times*. But the Treasury could only advise. The decision is the Prime Minister's, and since Alan Walters rather liked the idea of Haddon Cave ('Hong

Kong is the best-run government in the world') his chances were not to be taken lightly.

Eventually, Downing Street decided that the next Governor would have to be someone with an established City reputation, which Haddon Cave lacked. Scholey, Morse and McMahon were, indeed, passed over. Walters cannot remember exactly how the name of Robin Leigh-Pemberton, then the chairman of NatWest, arose: 'I like Robin. I may well have suggested him, and in the end we had no one else to choose from,' he reports. Mrs Thatcher knew him a little and liked him too. But when the appointment was revealed to the Treasury only hours before it was made public on 23 December 1982, Treasury ministers and civil servants assumed it was the Prime Minister's revenge on the Bank. 'I thought he would be a figurehead and a tool of the professionals,' says one of the Treasury ministers.

There had been one other candidate, who offered himself not long before the decision was taken. This was Gordon Richardson. He proposed a shortened term of two or three years to allow him to continue his work on the debt crisis. The Prime Minister was not interested. As far as she was concerned, his time was up, as was indicated by the honours that were lavished upon him. Apart from accepting membership of the Privy Council, which allowed him to share secrets with ministers, the Governor had deliberately refused honours during his ten years at the Bank. He was Mr Gordon Richardson.

In the 1983 New Year's Honours list he was made a life peer, and took the title of Lord Richardson of Duntisbourne in the County of Gloucestershire. Then Buckingham Palace announced his appointment as a Knight Companion of the Garter. As exits go, few are more splendid.

8

The Romance of Central Banking

A year earlier Gordon Richardson had been elected to a post that must have given him no less pleasure than the Queen's award of the Garter; possibly more. He had been unanimously acclaimed by the few men in the world who were his peers – the heads of the central banks of ten leading industrial nations. Richardson had been elected chairman of the governors' committee that met each month in Basle at the Bank for International Settlement, the central bankers' central bank. He succeeded Jelle Zijlstra, the illustrious President of the Netherlands central bank, and although he was already the senior man at the time, his election had nothing to do with Buggins's turn. It sprang from a genuine respect for the Governor's experience and authority. That might have been undermined in London by the Prime Minister, her attendant shoal of Thatcherites and even some cheeky civil servants, but in Basle it was undiminished.

Richardson missed only one of the monthly meetings at the BIS in his decade as Governor. He enjoyed Basle, where he was among men who trusted each other and did not need to watch their tongues. The director of the Bank's overseas department, Anthony Loehnis, comments: 'Among friends, they let their hair down about their political masters.' On summer evenings they would sit together on the terrace of the Hotel Schweitzerhof over a nightcap. Journalists were unwelcome intruders. It was the one place in the world where you could be sure to see Richardson laughing.

The Bank of England's role at Basle reflected the prestige of the overseas department. This rests on a tradition that began in the 1920s, when Montagu Norman enjoyed the power and intrigue of confidential work undertaken on behalf of the League of Nations. His activities sometimes sound like an outline for a John Buchan novel, as when he helped save the Austrian economy from collapse in 1921 – an episode described by Arthur Salter, secretary of the League's financial committee at the time.

> In our opinion there was only one man in Europe who could do it – Montagu Norman. His position was then unique in prestige and influence. There was only one doubt in my mind: will Norman want to help? . . . I was convinced that nothing less than direct intervention would save Austria from disintegrating in utter ruin; and if that happened Italy and Czechoslovakia would step in. Each of these countries had designs on Austria, but at the time they were jealous of one another. Neither, it seemed to Blackett of the Treasury

and me, would be willing to move unless to thwart the other. Blackett thought a big loan might tide Austria over if her currency, revenue and commerce were rationalized, and I agreed to approach Norman.

The Governor was intrigued and immediately sympathetic. He promised to see what he could do and keep me closely informed. I was impressed by his grasp of the many tangled issues . . . If it hadn't been for Norman's stage management, the League could have done little. He got no public credit for it because he worked as usual through others behind the scenes. He wasn't the kind of man who sought praise for doing what he regarded as his job as a central banker.

Norman was just as fond of the BIS as Richardson. He had hoped its constitution would create a body of bankers that was entirely free of governments, and even when that proved to be an illusion, he still put his personal stamp on the institution. His biographer, Andrew Boyle, writes that Basle was Norman's 'spiritual home away from home' and records a description of the Governor by one of the BIS staff in 1930s.

Norman's prestige in Basle was overwhelming. As the apostle of central bank cooperation, he made the central banker into a kind of arch-priest of monetary religion. The BIS was in fact his creation. He came on Saturday morning, and left on Monday morning, accompanied by his retinue. The other governors flocked to his room . . . Public opinion thought he pursued political aims, even sinister ones during his visits to Basle . . . This I am convinced was all imagination. But Norman strongly believed in the political importance of close cooperation between central bankers in their own domain.

So did Gordon Richardson, and the overseas department retained an élite position inside the Bank even after its role had changed fundamentally. It had always taken a higher proportion of graduates than any other and its best jobs for bright young men were in Washington DC, where by tradition the private secretary to the managing director of the IMF is appointed by the Bank. Much of the economic intelligence read in Whitehall comes from members of the overseas department, who are stationed in capitals like Tokyo, or who have just returned from a trip through Africa or the Middle East. Its reputation survived the radical changes in its role that followed the decision to allow sterling to float in 1973, and to wind up the sterling area in 1976. Its influence overseas had already been affected by the transition of British colonies into the Commonwealth, but the Bank had left its mark all over the world, providing governors and foreign-exchange controllers for a large proportion of the newly established central banks that had sprung up after independence was granted to British colonies. There is still the odd trace of the old days, like a seat on the Cayman Island Currency Board; a Bank man flies out to the Caribbean, religiously, twice a year to attend to these duties.

President Jimmy Carter turned to the Bank in 1980 when he needed an intermediary to discuss the return of frozen Iranian assets in the United States as a prelude to the release of American hostages in Tehran. The probity of the Bank made it acceptable to the Ayatollahs, though it occasionally exasperated the President. During a delay, while Kit McMahon of the Bank satisfied himself about the final financial procedures, the President exploded: 'What are they doing? Writing it out with a goddam quill pen?'

Such overseas adventures are a tonic after months spent in Threadneedle Street tinkering with the monetary system or analysing economic statistics. The romance of central banking, it seems, begins at Heathrow Airport, and just before Richardson retired he was plunged into one of the classic experiences of modern central banking – the international debt crisis. Montagu Norman would have envied the part played in that by Richardson, who made no more public fuss about it than Norman would have done, but who equally quietly revelled in it.

The overseas department had already studied the conditions that were likely to cause a debt crisis somewhere, sometime soon. Following the eruption of the oil price in 1973 and 1979, commercial banks had more money to lend than they knew what to do with, and what many did with it was certain to be rash. Capital poured out of the Middle East into countries with an inexhaustible appetite for new money, like Mexico, Brazil and Argentina. This flow was encouraged, of course, by the leading industrial countries and the I M F as a means of keeping up the level of international economic activity. This was 'recycling' and one of its consequences was a real-estate boom not confined to South American countries, for it spread to cities like New York, where billions of the dollars intended for South and Central America were actually spent. Sovereign debt held many commercial banks in thrall to unstable governments like Zaïre. The oil price began to level out in 1980 and from late 1981 the OPEC oil producers were borrowing more than they were lending. Richardson, speaking to the Overseas Bankers Club in London in February 1983, assented to the proposition that given the state of the world economy, the rate of international bank lending reached by 1981 had become unsustainable. Moreover, he continued, the borrowers' thirst for capital was so great that too drastic a reduction in international lending would cause an insupportable burden of adjustment. The banks, in others words, had lent too much, but could not now afford to stop lending. Given that analysis, the only questions were: when would the crisis break, and where? The answer was the summer of 1982, in Mexico.

There were tremors beforehand: a devaluation of the peso in the spring, and the closure of the currency markets in August; but the crisis broke, as if it had been managed by a stage director, at the annual meeting of the World Bank and IMF, held that year in Toronto in the first week of September. All the players were there. The Mexicans were threatening to suspend payments on international loans. The banks that had lent the money countered with threats of legal action to obtain repayment of the loans. Each was making a potential victim of the other, and no one was sure of the consequences, except that they could be dire. One danger of a Mexican default was that other debtor nations might follow suit and should they do so, confidence in the international loan market between banks (the inter-bank market) would drain away. That might virtually halt international borrowing and lending, and the whole banking system would be put at risk.

If it could be as bad as that, some big men were required to prevent it happening, and they were on hand in Toronto. Among the central bankers and the chiefs of the IMF two men stood out: Richardson, of course, and Paul Volcker, the commanding chairman of the Governors of the Federal Reserve, the man who had survived mortal combat with inflation in the United States. (One of his weapons had been high interest rates, a reason why debtor nations found interest payments such a burden.) The two men shared a conviction that it is the duty of central bankers to save governments and markets from the worst of their mistakes, and although neither communicates very freely, each understood the other, speaking in an oblique shorthand based on shared assumptions and an appreciation of the dangers involved. They went into private session in Richardson's suite, and

133

woe betide any unauthorized visitor who interrupted them. (Two alarmed French bankers were ejected by Volcker personally.)

The first move was to quell the agitation before it turned into panic. That meant persuading Mexico to pay interest on its short-term debts in London and New York, while they arranged to reschedule the original loans. Next the commercial banks had to be kept in line. If one bank had pulled the plug on a short-term Mexican loan, or had begun a legal action to force repayment of the principal, the rest might well have followed suit. Richardson and Volcker were able to prevent a panic in Toronto, but that was only a start. During the next few months they had to deploy the whole range of central-banking techniques to deal with the crisis, among them cooperation, conciliation, persuasion, flattery and resuscitation – all in the strictest confidence.

The commercial banks, meeting in New York to deal with the crisis, and looking nervously over their shoulders at the reactions of their competitors, made it clear that they would feel more secure if Volcker and Richardson appointed representatives, to hold their hands as it were. This request for cooperation brought new faces on to the scene, Richardson nominating a small, fierce-looking Glaswegian, Brian Quinn, the antithesis of an old Bank man. His father was a shipyard worker who had played for Celtic as an amateur and who had won the Glasgow billiards championship. Quinn had trained as an economist and worked at the IMF before joining the Bank, where he succeeded by becoming an accessible and candid press officer. Richardson trusted him and had promoted him to the assistant directorship of the banking-supervision department.

What marked Quinn out as a central banker was an unusual degree of commitment. Listening to the commercial bankers in New York haggling over details and even questioning whether the Mexican debt crisis was capable of a solution, Quinn told them politely but with some vigour to pull themselves together, and consider the consequences of a failure to agree. This proved effective – until the next emergency.

Those banks that were not represented in New York also showed signs of nerves, which was the signal for the Bank and the Federal Reserve to turn to the central bankers' old-boy network. For example, when an Italian bank threatened to withdraw its money from Mexico, Richardson telephoned the Governor of the Bank of Italy to ask him to lean personally on the potential transgressor. The network produced immediate results everywhere except Singapore, whose central bank at first piously declined to take any responsibility for the profligate ways of Central American nations. Richardson had to use his full weight to impress upon them the importance of their cooperation. What they learned from Richardson was that unless they did the favour he asked for now, they could expect absolutely no favours at all from the Bank of England or the Federal Reserve in the future.

Flattery was another persuasive device. At a vital stage in the negotiations, the commercial banks took umbrage at the IMF's high-handed manner and talked about withdrawing from the scheme that was being prepared. This was not an occasion to make threats: instead Richardson invited the chairmen of the major British banks to dinner. The best silver and the finest linen was brought out, and the guest list included the leading central bankers from Switzerland and the United States, as well as the managing director of the IMF in conciliatory mood. Shortly afterwards the British and the American banks with most at stake in Mexico reached an agreement to reschedule that nation's debts, a model agreement of its kind. The banks lost no more money than they deserved for having lent so rashly in the first place; the markets were intact; and so was Mexico – for another four years anyway.

The agreement was sewn up before Richardson left the Bank. Although he was willing to admit that the crisis had been exciting, like Norman saving the Austrian economy in 1921, he did not want too much made of it. What he had done was the essence of central banking. He had done it with great skill, however, and Volcker talked afterwards about the lucky coincidence that had brought them together to deal with the crisis. Richardson's international reputation was at its zenith.

He did not retire to cultivate his garden when he left the Bank in June 1983, but remained an imposing presence at meetings of world bankers, though posterity may view his achievements less respectfully than his colleagues in Basle did. Montagu Norman's reputation, for instance, is no longer based on his striking presence at BIS meetings, but on what happened during the Depression in Britain. Gordon Richardson could suffer a similar fate, and be better thought of abroad than at home.

9

Johnson Matthey Bankers:
the Horrors Begin

Robin Leigh-Pemberton says: 'I am by nature an optimist.' Since his birth on 5 January 1927 he has had a great deal to be optimistic about. His father owned 2,500 acres near Sittingbourne in Kent. His wife's mother was a stepdaughter-in-law of the Marquis of Exeter (who, on a chariot of fire, won a gold medal at the 1924 Olympics). Leigh-Pemberton went to Eton, where he showed academic promise; he was good at mathematics and better at classics, winning a scholarship to Trinity College, Oxford. He went to university after three years in the Guards: 'I was lucky enough to be in a very good battalion of the Grenadiers – it taught me a lot about leadership.'

After Oxford he became a barrister and, following a few uneventful years at the Bar, he returned to his Kentish property and became a country gentleman. His wife's stepfather-in-law asked him to become a director of Birmid Qualcast, a company that manufactures lawn mowers. Later Leigh-Pemberton was to say that nepotism might have got him his seat on the board, but not the chairmanship, which he achieved ten years later. Among other posts he held were those of leader of the Conservative group on the County Council, member of the committee of the County Cricket Club, pro-Chancellor of the University of Kent, a deputy Lord-Lieutenant, and a member of the local board of the NatWest. From there he was asked to join NatWest's board in 1972.

He clearly made an impression on his NatWest colleagues: in 1974 he was made executive vice-chairman and two years later chairman. His charm and agreeable nature made him a popular figure, and in 1982 he was asked to take over as chairman of the Committee of London Clearing Banks, making him the chief lobbyist for the clearing banks in Whitehall and Westminster, where he became acquainted with politicians and civil servants, and first met the Prime Minister and economic advisors like Alan Walters. With a fine house in Kent, five sons grown up, and on the verge of becoming Lord-Lieutenant of Kent, life must have seemed sweet, and his optimistic nature entirely justified. Then he was appointed Governor of the Bank of England.

The reception of this announcement would have come as a blow to the most cheerful nature. The tone was set by the leader column of the *Financial Times*: 'The failure to choose a successor to Gordon Richardson with greater experience and standing both in international and domestic banking circles is a cause for concern.' The Governor-designate then proceeded to shoot himself in the foot. Just as the

Mexican debt settlement was announced in December 1982, he stated his views of the world financial crisis. 'The international banking scene is my most immediate challenge,' he said. That was unexceptionable, but he continued: 'I think the crisis is over, if there ever was a crisis.' He did admit that 'there is a very serious situation which will take several years to solve', but the news that travelled was that the next Governor of the Bank of England considered there had never been an international debt crisis. (Richardson's advice to his successor had been that he refrain from comment on international finance until he had played himself in.) For his part, Richardson's old ally Denis Healey lost no time in putting the boot in, and declaring that Leigh-Pemberton was insufficiently experienced in international banking.

Within a month of the announcement of his appointment, Leigh-Pemberton had upset right-wingers by suggesting that inflation was infinitely more threatening to western democracy than communism; and left-wingers by the statement that he would resist any future Labour government's proposal to devalue the pound. It was very soon clear that the new Governor was not in the same mould as Richardson. That should have come as no surprise; since Mrs Thatcher did not want another proud and egotistical man at the Bank, she had appointed someone with the qualities of a good chairman. The executive directors who would still be working in Threadneedle Street after Richardson left in June 1983 took note of the change in the character of the Governor, and acted accordingly.

A few weeks before Robin Leigh-Pemberton took up his new post, an important new committee had been announced. Titled the Deputy Governor's Committee, its members were the executive and associate directors, who began to meet each Friday under the chairmanship of Kit McMahon. Its establishment created a distinction between the duties of the Governor, acting as the Bank's public spokesman, and the executive management of the day-to-day activities of the Bank. McMahon, under Richardson, had sometimes felt, frustratedly, that his abundant energy was under-used. Now he seized the opportunity to extend the compass of the deputy governorship. His new committee was a formal affair with an agenda and minutes, and for some time Leigh-Pemberton had access to neither. But, unlike Richardson, the new Governor did not keep highly paid officials waiting in the corridor, and when he was asked for a decision, he made up his mind pleasingly quickly. The staff, from the chief doorkeeper to the deputy governor, liked him without reservation. None the less, it was difficult to show that he was being treated as anything other than a figurehead.

Day-to-day decisions in the money markets were reported to him and he quickly mastered the jargon, but this was a period of calm in the Bank's relationship with the Treasury, and there were no radical decisions to be taken or troublesome corners to be fought. The City's institutions, especially the Stock Exchange, which was coming to terms with the prospect of fundamental reorganization, were a continuing interest of his, but areas like banking supervision were technical and could be left to the technicians.

The supervisors had much to say for themselves, and the Deputy Governor's Committee often discussed complaints from the banking-supervision department about staff shortages. The spread of the Mexican debt crisis to other Central and South American countries forced the supervisors to spend more time pondering the balance-sheets of large, first-tier – or 'recognized' – banks than had ever been intended. The minutes of the Deputy Governor's Committee would show, however, that its members were intent on running a tight ship, and requests for more manpower were turned down.

The banking-supervision department was also unhappy about the Banking Act, 1979. The faults in the two-tier system which they had spotted while it was being assembled had turned into serious weaknesses. There were recognized banks that were clearly in need of greater attention than the Act required or the Bank had time to give. The supervisors wanted revisions in the Act, and early in 1984 the Deputy Governor's Committee agreed to prepare the necessary papers, so that serious discussions with the Treasury could begin. The first meeting between the Bank and the Treasury took place in May 1984, and more were planned. But none of the participants felt any great urgency.

The supervisors were not worried merely by the two-tier system. Among themselves, they admitted concern over declining standards of prudence and probity in the banking industry. The standards supervisors upheld were not explicitly stated in the Banking Act. For years the Bank had volunteered the advice given to US banks in 1863 by a Comptroller of the Currency named Hugh McCulloch, which had lost none of its relevance in the ensuing 120 years. The Bank had had McCulloch's words printed and hung, framed, on the wall of the waiting-room in the banking-supervision department. Since the advice is appropriate, it is worth repeating much of it here.

Let no loans be made that are not secured beyond a reasonable contingency. Do nothing to foster and encourage speculation. Give facilities only to legitimate and prudent transactions . . .

Distribute your loans rather than concentrate them in a few hands. Large loans to a single individual or firm, although sometimes proper and necessary, are generally injudicious and frequently unsafe. Large borrowers are apt to control the bank; and when this is the relation between a bank and its customers, it is not difficult to decide which in the end will suffer. Every dollar that a bank loans above its capital and surplus it owes for, and its managers are therefore under the strongest obligation to its creditors, as well as to its stockholders, to keep its discounts constantly under control . . .

Treat your customers liberally, bearing in mind the fact that a bank prospers as its customers prosper, but never permit them to dictate your policy.

If you doubt the propriety of discounting an offering, give the bank the benefit of the doubt and decline it; never make a discount if you doubt the propriety of doing it. If you have reasons to distrust the integrity of a customer, close his account. Never deal with a rascal under the impression that you can prevent him from cheating you. The risk in such cases is greater than the profits.

Pay your officers such salaries as will enable them to live comfortably and respectably without stealing; and require of them their entire services. If an officer lives beyond his income, dismiss him; even if his excess expenditure can be explained consistent with his integrity, still dismiss him. Extravagance, if not a crime, very naturally leads to crime. A man cannot be a safe officer of the bank who spends more than he earns.

Pursue a straightforward, upright, legitimate banking business. Never be tempted by the prospect of large returns to do anything but what may be properly be done under [the law]. 'Splendid financiering' is not legitimate banking, and 'splendid financiers' in banking are generally either humbugs or rascals.

It was unfortunate that the directors of Johnson Matthey Bankers Ltd did not read this sage advice before September 1984. Before then they had studiously ignored virtually every single rule. Johnson Matthey encouraged and fostered speculation, concentrated loans in a few large hands, dealt with rascals, failed to dismiss officers

who lived beyond their means, became involved in 'splendid financiering' and pursued a course that entirely ignored straightforward,
upright, legitimate banking business. The only respect in which
Johnson Matthey might be said to have met McCulloch's requirements
was that it treated its customers liberally.

The Chancellor of the Exchequer, Nigel Lawson, described the
story of Johnson Matthey Bankers as an 'appalling and bizarre record
of incompetence and mismanagement'. Labour MPs like Brian
Sedgemore and Dennis Skinner declared that it was a fraud and that it
was the Bank of England's fault. Both called for an inquiry and the
resignation of the Governor. The inquiry that took place was not the
sort they hoped for, and the Governor did not consider resignation,
but the JMB affair was the most damaging incident in the history of
the Bank since Montagu Norman and Winston Churchill fell out in 1927
after the return to the Gold Standard. Relations with the Chancellor
and the Treasury were worse than they had been in 1980, and Lawson
did not hesitate to censure the Bank in the Commons. Confidence
among the staff in Threadneedle Street was badly damaged and the
Bank's mystique crumbled like some ancient artefact suddenly exposed
to air and light. The affair changed the way the institution was
regarded, both inside and outside the Bank.

How did the JMB affair happen? Johnson Matthey belongs in
Hatton Garden, where it has been in the precious-metals business since
1817. By 1984 it employed 6,000 people, mainly in the Home Counties
– another 4,000 worked in foreign subsidiaries. In London the company
was best known as a bullion dealer, one of the five members of the
London gold fixing, the group that meets twice a day at Rothschilds
Bank to fix a world price for gold. But the company was also a refiner
of precious metals, and manufactured a number of products like
jewellery, catalysts containing platinum, and electrical contacts containing silver. Its banking subsidiary had opened for business in 1965;
they moved out of Hatton Garden to Fenchurch Street, and their
colleagues on the bullion side let them get on with it.

Membership of the gold fixing gave Johnson Matthey a presence
in the City. It was authorized by the Bank to deal in foreign exchange
in 1967 and was exempted from the Protection of Depositors Act – as
all proper banks had to be – in 1970. When the two-tier system in the
Banking Act was introduced there was no question about JMB's position: it was placed in the first tier, as a recognized bank that would be

142

only lightly supervised compared with the licensed deposit takers in the second tier. At the time, most of its business involved bullion, and the 1980 accounts showed that of total assets of £874 million, holdings of bullion and customers' bullion-related accounts came to £678 million. The banking business – commercial loans and overdrafts – amounted to no more than £34 million. All but one million of Johnson Matthey's £14.4 million profits were attributable to the precious-metals business. When the main board of Johnson Matthey declared that the banking side had some catching up to do, the directors adopted a bolder lending policy. JMB submitted the required statistical information, and when the Bank's supervisors had analysed them management was informed that its capital ratios were quite adequate. The Bank's own account of the JMB affair (published in its 1985 Annual Report) says: 'even allowing for the nature of the business, the capital ratios left room on the Bank's normal criteria for an appreciable expansion of the balance-sheet'. The subsequent expansion was rather greater than 'appreciable', however, as the table shows (figures are millions of pounds):

(at end March)	1980	1981	1982	1983	1984
Loans and overdrafts	34	78	135	184	309
Holdings of bullion and customer-related accounts	678	786	804	1,226	1,359
Total assets	874	1,040	1,183	1,735	2,089

Other forms of trade finance – letters of credit, guarantees and outstanding acceptances – rose quickly too: from £18 million in 1980 to £65 million in 1984. Indeed, the only item on the balance-sheet that did not grow annually was profits, as the next table shows (figures in millions of pounds):

(year to end March)	1980	1981	1982	1983	1984
Pre-tax profits	14.4	11.6	16.6	24.3	9.4
Made up from dealing (including bullion)	13.4	10.0	14.7	20.8	8.9
Banking	1.0	1.6	1.9	3.5	0.5

The Bank's supervisors first took a special look at JMB in 1983, though what interested them was not the banking business but the bullion trading. During the early 1980s trading in gold and silver had been frenetic. This was an aberrant period when the Hunts of Dallas and some Saudi princes had tried to corner the silver market, and a wave of political hysteria in the Middle East had forced the price of gold to $825 an ounce. A few New York bullion dealers had made profits of hundreds of millions of dollars dealing in precious metals. (For instance, Phillip Brothers, known as Phibro, made enough to buy the investment bankers, Salomon Brothers.) Other bullion dealers lost so heavily that they limped away from the business altogether. JMB survived the period – no more, no less. In the trade it was considered unsophisticated. Other traders boasted that it was possible to buy from one subsidiary of Johnson Matthey and sell to another, Johnson Matthey Commodities, and make a nice profit. None of the imaginative new trading instruments, like options, which other bullion dealers introduced to keep business going when the market-place became over-crowded, were available from JMB. There was talk of a merger with Ansbacher's merchant bank, but enthusiasm for that subsided – perhaps after a careful scrutiny of the accounts.

In 1983 the Bank was concerned about JMB's liquidity position, but this then improved; and when the supervisors returned to express disquiet about loans made by the Commodities subsidiary, the amount lent by JMB was reduced. Putting these two matters right took three meetings between JMB's management and the Bank's supervisors, but the real trouble, when it began, involved neither of these issues. Instead, it was the banking business, where there should have been no problems, since a footnote in the annual report for the year ended 31 March 1984 stated explicitly: 'Provision is made for all known doubtful debts.' Such a provision was, of course, prudent commercial banking.

The Bank explained what happened next: 'In 1984 problems began to arise with two large exposures. JMB was faced with the familiar banker's dilemma of deciding whether to lend more to help the customer trade out of its problems or to refuse further credit and bring about the customer's failure. JMB chose the former course.'

Put like that, JMB sounds merely like a large clearing bank taking a decision not to bankrupt a local manufacturing business. Indeed, the Bank had recommended exactly that course of action to the clearers in the early 1980s during the darkest days of the British industrial recession. But JMB was not the same as other banks. The difference between JMB and other banks was that in the six months between April and September 1984 the total loan book had increased by over one third, and a large proportion of the money lent had gone to a very small number of customers. In March 1984, two customers borrowed sums so large that they amounted to 65 per cent and 34 per cent of the bank's capital base. By September these had risen to 76 per cent and 39 per cent respectively. If the borrowers had been I C I and G E C this would have been defensible, if still somewhat imprudent. But J M B was too new to the scene to have developed that sort of business, which anyway would not have been profitable enough. (I C I can squeeze a banker's margin so tightly that the business often seems hardly worth having.) What J M B wanted was a comfortable spread (the difference between the cost of borrowing money and the price of lending it). Businessmen who are willing to pay one or two points above normal interest rates are the sort of customers who are not always welcomed by large London and New York banks. Moreover, J M B had a singular advantage: a name that was familiar in parts of the world where bullion is big business, and Johnson Matthey $3\frac{3}{4}$ ounce gold bars are common currency – that is, the Indian subcontinent and the Arabian Gulf.

The bank's largest customer was a Pakistani shipowner named Mahmoud Sipra, whose friends called him 'the cobra' (with friends like that it hardly mattered that his enemies called him 'the devil'). Sipra's group was El Saeed, and J M B lent money to a number of associated companies within the group. Not all of it went into shipping, for Sipra had ambitions in the film industry, which were not cheaply satisfied. To allow him to live in the style to which he wished to become accustomed, he bought the fine house in Regent's Park that had belonged to the late Sir Ralph Richardson. A flamboyant figure, he had come to the attention of people in the shipping business, who later contributed ammunition for the use of the Labour M P for Hackney, Brian Sedgemore, when he prosecuted the case against J M B in the Commons. An investigator in maritime fraud, for example, reported to Sedgemore that he had approached J M B in 1982 and warned one of the directors, Ian Fraser, that Sipra was involved in a £3 million fraud claim. Fraser had shown no interest, Sedgemore alleged in the Commons.

J M B seemed to have no reservations about Abdul Shamji either. He had arrived in London in 1972 as a refugee from Idi Amin, though not penniless. His group, called Gomba, after a village in Uganda, had assets of more than £1 million. As Gomba grew during the next ten

145

years it became clear that Shamji's greatest skill was not making profits, since the group reported a loss in its first seven years, but making friends and borrowing money. His business philosophy was simple: 'You don't have to have a bank balance to be rich. You just have to persuade the banks to lend you money.' When making friends, however, it helped to have money. Having donated to its funds, Shamji became a vice-president of an advice centre called the Small Business Bureau, whose objectives fitted neatly into Mrs Thatcher's philosophy. On the wall of his office in Park Lane hung a photograph of the Prime Minister speaking at a dinner given by Shamji. Norman Tebbit, when he was Secretary of State for Trade and Industry, was another Conservative friend. A couple of Tory MPs gave paid advice and helped smooth Shamji's way – not always an easy task, for while Shamji was able to ingratiate himself with the higher reaches of the political establishment, he found it extremely difficult to turn a profit from his businesses.

Buying a truck-manufacturing company called Stonefield, located in Cumnock, near Glasgow, Shamji was hailed as an entrepreneur whose intervention had saved Scottish jobs. Mrs Thatcher was pictured sitting in the cab of a Stonefield truck, but her magic failed to rub off on the sales figures. In 1983 Shamji moved the business to Kent, leaving no evidence of his company's existence in Scotland but a trail of unpaid bills. Once in the south, he omitted to pay the Inland Revenue the income tax he had already deducted from his employees' wages. He was, by nature, a spender rather than a payer.

The only place where Gomba did manage to turn a profit apparently was in Nigeria, where it could be done by knowing the right people. One of Shamji's new friends was the man who ran the state government in Anambia, who became a partner in a Gomba subsidiary named Greenfield Construction. He awarded construction contracts to Greenfield – which was well named, since the sites of the roads, bridges and flyovers it had been contracted to build were still green fields years later. Money for this work had changed hands, however, and when after a coup the state government was indicted, £3 million turned out to be the sum that had changed hands for work not done.

In 1984 Shamji began a policy of spending his way out of trouble. This spree netted him three West End theatres and Wembley Stadium. But judged by past experience, his prospects in the property business were not promising. Gomba owned Alford House in Park Lane, which produced an annual income of £310,000. To enable it to be used as security for new bank loans, Shambi had inflated its value, and interest payments on the money borrowed with Alford House as security came to £600,000 a year, the difference being made up by fresh loans. Of these, £22 million came from JMB, which was among Shamji's most generous benefactors and some of whose directors were among his friends.

Rajendra Sethia's ambition was to be the richest Indian in the world, a conceit he had developed in Calcutta, where he had grown up as a member of one of the leading commercial families. At the London School of Economics, where he studied, no one seems to have taught him about prudence, and shortly after leaving it, Sethia discovered how quickly money could be made in commodities trading. He established ESAL Commodities, and developed a close trading relationship with Nigeria, specializing in sugar, and spending his profits on a white Rolls-Royce and a large house in north London. ESAL's speculative and trading activities were financed by bank loans, of course, the largest lenders being the Punjab National Bank and the Central Bank of India: but the list of Sethia's bankers included JMB, which had provided him with nearly £6 million by the time ESAL Commodities went bankrupt – owing £170 million, a British all-comers' record.

Those three 'splendid financiers' were JMB's main customers, but there was a host of small fry to whom the bank was also obliging – English businessmen like Michael Hepker, who was lent £1½ million to develop a site. This sounds secure enough – except that, as Sedgemore told the Commons, planning permission had already been withdrawn when the loan was made. The record shows that Johnson Matthey Bankers was a remarkably easy touch. The important question is: when did the record show this? It is, after all, the job of Bank of England supervisors to regulate this kind of 'splendid financiering'.

The operations of the supervision department are split between analysts and managers. Analysts handle statistical returns from banks and licensed deposit takers and prepare reports. Departmental etiquette allows them to sign letters of acknowledgement, but nothing more substantial. Acting on the analysts' reports is a team of managers, each of whom is responsible for a number of banks. Normally, they meet their subjects at the Bank, but if he or she spots a weakness in the balance-sheet, the manager will visit the bankers on their home ground. (The reason why bankers usually visit the Bank rather than supervisors visiting them is fear of City gossip; until recently, a visit from the Bank meant bad news.)

The manager whose portfolio included JMB had identified problems of weak liquidity and excessive lending to the commodities subsidiaries after personal visits to the bank the previous winter. These faults had been corrected, but the flaws they revealed in the management suggested JMB justified permanent and close scrutiny. In the vital months from March to August 1984, it did not get it.

One plausible explanation is that the managers in the supervision department were dangerously overworked. Problems of understaffing, many of the managers felt, were exacerbated by a lack of leadership. The assistant director for banking supervision was Brian Quinn, who had joined the department in 1982. He had been promoted to the job with the unwritten instruction that he should sort it out, but almost every week in the last part of 1982 and for most of 1983 Quinn took a Concorde flight to New York to attend meetings about the debt crisis, returning on Concorde the same evening. When he finally returned to the department full-time early in 1984, he succumbed to shingles, which disabled him for a month.

His immediate chief was the associate director for banking supervision, Peter Cooke, who was also chairman of the BIS committee of bank supervisors from ten of the leading industrial nations. (It was actually called the Cooke Committee.) Cooke had joined the Bank from Oxford and developed a taste for international economic administration, working in Basle at the BIS and in Washington DC at the IMF. The supervisors' committee in Basle seemed the perfect niche for his talents, but meant that he was often away from his office in the Parlours. When he was there, he was not easily approachable. In 1984, after thirty years in Threadneedle Street, he qualified as an old Bank man and might have begun to take deference from his junior staff for granted. He was not the sort to whom a troubled manager often felt like taking a problem.

The manager who had the JMB file had other things on her mind. (The Bank asked me not to identify her because she has experienced enough anguish, and since the point of this story is not actually served by doing so, I agreed not to.) Another of her files was Continental Illinois, the Chicago bank still recovering from near collapse a year earlier. It had had to be bailed out by the American authorities, having lent imprudently in the oil and gas business. Monitoring the fall-out from Continental Illinois might easily have been a full-time job for a supervisor, but there were not enough to go round. JMB ought to have been full time, except that the supervisor had not been able to identify exactly what was wrong at the bank.

The analysts were expecting JMB's report for the quarter ending March 1984 by the middle of April, but it did not arrive. JMB having been pressed on several occasions, the March return finally arrived in the middle of June. Since the two largest exposures were increasing in size, the news was disturbing. In December 1983 Sipra was reported to have borrowed a sum equal to 27 per cent of JMB's capital base: by June 1984, that had risen to 42 per cent. The amount lent to Sethia and his friends was up from 18 per cent to 30 per cent. The March return also revealed for the first time another large exposure, amounting to 14 per cent of the capital. Sophisticated analysis was hardly needed to conclude that it was time for another meeting with JMB – at their office, rather than the Bank. The manager requested a meeting in July. JMB held out for August, to which the manager agreed. By the time the meeting took place, early in August, JMB's return for the June quarter had arrived. The paperwork suggested that Sipra exposure had fallen to 38 per cent of the capital base, while Sethia and allies were up to 34 per cent, and another new customer had loans amounting to 17 per cent of the capital. When the supervisor inquired into the identity of the new customer it turned out to be Sipra, by another company name. Lumping his debts together brought them up to 55 per cent of the capital.

Nevertheless, the action taken by the Bank was precautionary rather than positive. After all, this was an authorized bank, and the Bank of England supervisors were not accustomed to busting in like the VAT-man. Instead, the Bank expressed serious concern about the concentration of loans in the hands of a few customers – none of whom fulfilled the definition of 'a good name' – and asked JMB's auditors to look at the loans more closely.

Hindsight is hardly necessary to recognize that JMB warranted more urgent and sceptical scrutiny than it received. Later it became clear that JMB's management had misinformed the Bank about the size of the loans to the two largest customers (Sipra having actually borrowed 76 per cent rather than 55 per cent, and the Sethia group 39 per cent, not 34 per cent, of the bank's capital). This transformed the diagnosis from dangerous to critical. The inaccurate statistics were themselves justification for direct intervention by the supervisors.

The Bank's response, however, revealed the trusting nature of its relations with authorized banks. Its practice had been to rely on the accuracy of their statistical returns, and to encourage bankers to bring their troubles to the attention of the Bank. In the case of JMB, the practice proved inadequate. Moreover, the supervisor had too much work. She discussed her cases with her colleagues, sharing her gloom about both Continental Illinois and JMB. The joke was: which would go first? But she did not share the joke with Brian Quinn. When JMB advised the Bank on Tuesday 25 September 1984 that their accountants, Arthur Young, had examined the two largest loans and found that they were not properly secured, the news was a shock for which the top men in the department were unprepared.

The Governor was in Washington at the time at the annual World Bank/IMF jamboree, along with a number of senior directors. Kit McMahon, who had an IMF committee to chair over the weekend before the formal meeting, returned to London overnight on Monday to take charge in Robin Leigh-Pemberton's absence. Shortly after his arrival on the morning of 25 September he learned there was a banking-supervision problem. At that stage, all that the supervisors could tell him was that substantial provisions – or write-offs – were required on the loans to Sipra, and Sethia and his allies. JMB's net worth would certainly be drastically reduced, but on that Tuesday it looked as though the problem was of liquidity. Insolvency did not seem likely.

The auditors, Arthur Young, were ordered to look at the books again, the Bank meanwhile mentioning the problem to the clearing banks, and suggesting it might be another occasion for a 'lifeboat', as in the 1974 secondary banking crisis. But McMahon's suggestion met with a frosty response. As far as the clearers were concerned, one sortie with a lifeboat was enough. By Thursday 27 September, however, this notion had become academic. Arthur Young had discovered many more bad loans; the problem was not one of liquidity; JMB was bust. Unless it was recapitalized, it would cease trading.

The main board of Johnson Matthey plc had been kept informed throughout the week, but the awful implications sank in only on the morning of Friday 29 September. Unless the banking subsidiary was bailed out, the whole of Johnson Matthey – refiners of precious metals, manufacturers of catalysts, contacts and costume jewellery – would come crashing down. If 6,000 jobs were to be saved, JMB itself must survive. But no right-minded bankers would take on JMB's losses as they were. Another firm of chartered accountants had been asked by the Bank for a second opinion, and the figures were appalling. The total loans by JMB came to £450 million: bad and doubtful loans seemed to amount to £250 million: but the bank's capital reserves were no more than about £120 million.

The major shareholder in Johnson Matthey plc was the Johannesburg mining conglomerate, Charter Consolidated. At the Bank's insistence, it injected £50 million of new capital into JMB, safeguarding its own investment in the parent company by making the bank a little more attractive to a purchaser. JMB did have some assets: it was a member of the London gold fixing, and it had a substantial bullion business that seemed clear of the infection that crippled the banking side. The search for a purchaser began on 29 September. The Bank first tried one of the clearers, with no success at all. Then a Canadian bank, the Bank of Nova Scotia, expressed an interest, and negotiations began in earnest.

The fact that the Bank was already looking for a buyer made it surprising to everyone that when the London markets closed that Friday the news of JMB's bust had not leaked. There was unease in the gold market, especially towards the end of the afternoon, when Robert Guy, bullion director at Rothschilds, telephoned the other members and asked them to be at the Bank at 9.30 the following morning – Saturday. From then on Kleinwort Benson (owners of Sharps Pixley), the Midland Bank (Samuel Montagu) and Standard Chartered (Mocatta and Goldsmid) knew that, whatever the secret might be, it involved the bullion market. The first rumours surfaced in New York later that day, and moved on with the clock to Hong Kong, where bullion traders work on Saturday, which was not the practice of the London market.

Michael Hawkes, chairman of Kleinwort Benson, recalls a tricky decision the following morning: 'What to wear to the Bank of England on a Saturday?' He chose his normal City suit, but as a concession to the weekend, a shirt that was less formal than usual. On learning about JMB's crisis, he and Evelyn Rothschild were particularly anxious about its effects on the gold market. They spelled out their worries to McMahon: the members of the fixing are bullion banks, a substantial proportion of whose liabilities are in the form of gold. Governments,

institutions and invididuals all over the world find it convenient to
keep their gold in London. They went on to explain a particularly
delicate point about the bullion business. A firm like J M B did not
keep all its customers' gold in the vaults. Some was leased to companies
that used gold in manufacturing processes. While the bullion bank was
solvent, there was never any problem in providing a customer with his
gold whenever it was requested, but if all the cusomers asked for the
return of their gold at the same time, there would not be enough to go
around.

As Hawkes and Rothschild pointed out, most individuals, banks
and governments assume that their gold exists in bullion bars in the
vaults under the City of London, but if J M B was not capable of
returning, physically, the gold that clients had deposited with it, that
comfortable assumption would be exploded. The clients of other,
solvent, bullion banks, wishing to protect themselves against a similar
misfortune, would then rush to withdraw their bullion, and if there
was not enough gold, the gold market – a fragile, almost illusory
institution – would collapse. The soundness of institutions like
Kleinworts and Rothschilds would be threatened. And that was only
the beginning of the bad news.

With confidence in the bullion banks gone, the calamity would
spread to the British banking system. Behind their hands, they whis-
pered the name of one of the clearers – the Midland Bank, whose
American subsidiary, the Crocker National Bank of San Francisco,
was in dire straits. McMahon recalled the crisis at Continental Illinois,
when massive amounts of money had moved from U S banks in general
into Britain, Europe and Japan. The failure of J M B risked provoking
a similar flight away from British banks, and possibly sterling too. The
point the bullion men were making had been taken, but the negotiations with the Bank of Nova Scotia were promising. They did not
founder until Sunday afternoon. The Canadians feared that legal
complications might set in if they bought J M B and, since no one was
able to indemnify the Bank of Nova Scotia against lawsuits, the
negotiations terminated. Not only was it a grave disappointment to
McMahon and to Johnson Matthey plc, it now presented them with a
deadline. At 2 a.m. on Monday morning, London time, the market
would open in Hong Kong, where J M B had a bullion-dealing subsidiary. A decision would have to be taken about whether that company
should open or not and there were only nine hours in which to take it.

The Bank telephoned the board of Johnson Matthey plc and executives from Charter Consolidated, from the bullion bankers and the clearers, and Price Waterhouse, the accountants. They were all asked to come back to the Bank at 6.30 p.m. on Sunday evening.

The Bank chose to direct the operation as though it were a French farce. The different parties were kept in separate rooms, and none was supposed to know that the others were there. As groups were ushered into McMahon's office, and out again, some would wonder whether they had not glimpsed a familiar figure disappearing down a corridor. Michael Hawkes of Kleinwort Benson at one stage slipped out of his room to explore: 'In one room there were the Johnson Matthey Bankers' books, and I spent a glorious two hours going through them. There wasn't a single name I'd ever heard of, and the amounts – £60 million to one name, £30 million to another – were absolutely staggering. We spent ages hanging around, lobbying every Bank of England man we could find and urging that Johnson Matthey must be rescued. Otherwise the gold market would go forthwith to Switzerland, and the malaise in the gold market might spread to other members of the market, perhaps even to the Midland Bank, who own Samuel Montagu. Till 10.30 at night all this seemed of no avail, and I came to the conclusion that the Bank of England had decided to let Johnson Matthey go.'

Having made that gloomy deduction, Hawkes told senior men whom he had ordered back to work in the London and Hong Kong offices to do all that was necessary to combat any threat of a run on Kleinworts when the news broke. There was a whiff of panic in the air. ('Where are the City's nerves of steel?' wondered one banker, listening to Rothschilds and Kleinworts.) The fearful bullion banks had agreed to contribute to a bail-out of JMB which would indemnify the purchaser against losses in the loan book, and at 10 p.m. had even agreed to McMahon's request for a bit more. Their contribution was still not enough.

By now McMahon faced a stark choice. The Bank could let JMB go, or it could save it. There was a case for letting it go. If JMB was bailed out every banker running a rotten loan book would conclude that when the going got rough, the Bank would bail him out too. Against that was the threat to the bullion banks and the possibility of a run on British banks generally. McMahon decided that the threat to the system was the greater, and that since no one else was willing to

153

shoulder the burden, the Bank would have to do so itself. But McMahon wanted to squeeze the others for as much help as he could. There was Charter Consolidated's £50 million for a start. The Bank was willing to contribute 10 per cent of the total sum, but felt that the clearing banks ought to contribute heavily to the indemnity fund. But they not only disagreed, they declared that they had already done the Bank enough favours. Since 1980, when they were asked not to call in loans made to ailing British manufacturers, they had felt that they had already bailed out half the industry in the West Midlands. J M B was a Bank of England problem, they told McMahon. Why, they asked, did the Bank not just move in and announce that J M B would be run by them? That ought to restore confidence. McMahon had to confess that the Bank had discovered a black hole in the Banking Act. A simple takeover was not permissible.

Eventually, the Bank of England reached a decision. Since it had no choice, it would have to buy J M B from Johnson Matthey plc. The purchase price was exactly one pound. This decision affected the clearers, and they agreed in principle to contribute to the indemnity fund. That was all they did agree during the night, however. The exact proportion they would contribute was to be decided in subsequent negotiations between the Bank and the clearers.

During the negotiations on Sunday night, the Governor, who had returned from the World Bank/I M F meeting in Washington D C, sat in his room, and by midnight, when the negotiations were sufficiently advanced, he called a special meeting of the Court to consent to the purchase. However, the details were not finalized by the time the Hong Kong market opened at 2 a.m. A telephone call went through to J M B's branch in Hong Kong, telling it not to open for business that morning and to pass the news on to Singapore. No explanation was given, but that message went much further than Singapore. Within minutes dealers in Sydney and Auckland knew too, and shortly after that the story was on the agency tapes and was being read all over south-east Asia. At 4 a.m. news flashed from Hong Kong that a number of reputable British banks, not just the bullion banks, had learned that some American and international banks with which they had strong links were refusing to do business.

For Kit McMahon, this was proof that he had done the right thing. The last task at the end of an exhausting weekend was to prepare the press notice that would be issued before the London markets opened that morning. It was a bland three paragraphs, mentioning 'problems' in the commercial lending book, consequent on which the Bank was 'acquiring' JMB. 'These arrangements enable Johnson Matthey Bankers to trade normally and meet all its commitments.' Though the announcement made the transaction sound as humdrum as possible, McMahon returned home feeling sick and a bit frightened. 'I foresaw all the horrors. It was easily the worst night of my life.'

10

A Drain on Spiritual Energy

For three weeks after the JMB crisis, the Bank seemed to have got away with it. Then, on 23 October 1984, Dennis Skinner, the left-wing Labour MP for the mining constituency of Bolsover, asked the Chancellor of the Exchequer a question about JMB. On the same day David Owen wrote the Chancellor a lengthy letter on the subject. These were the first hints of trouble in what was to turn into one of the City's most memorable scandals.

Four days after the Bank became the owner of JMB (effectively nationalizing it), three of its non-executive directors were sacked and a new chairman was named. This was Rodney Galpin, who had been head of the banking-supervision department in 1974. Within a week, Galpin had sacked the three leading executives, Roy Wheeler, James Firth and Ian Fraser, and recruited three experienced City men from Hambros Bank (Patrick Brenan), Charterhouse Japhet (Martin Harper) and Standard Chartered (L. T. G. Preston). The press statement announcing these changes added that the Bank's objective was to sell JMB as a going concern back into the private sector.

Skinner's question in the House was about the use of public funds in the rescue of JMB – a particularly emotional subject with him since the miners were on strike, ostensibly on that same issue (they wanted public funds used to keep unprofitable mines open). The Chancellor replied imperturbably that the Bank would be providing 'a small contribution' to the JMB indemnity fund. This idea that the Bank's contribution would be a modest one was echoed in the letter David Owen wrote to Nigel Lawson, which mentioned a contribution from the Bank of £10 million in terms that suggested he thought this much too high. But the main point of Dr Owen's letter was its emphasis on the state of the bullion market. The leader of the Social Democrats was renowned for his concern about the health service, his zeal for defence policy and foreign affairs, but he had never before written at length on the subject of gold. He had, however, only just met Dr Henry Jarecki.

It was a chance meeting during one of Jarecki's visits to London from New York, where he runs a company called Mocatta Metals. Through Jarecki's partnership with Standard Chartered Bank, which owned 32 per cent of Mocatta Metals, his business was intimately related to Mocatta and Goldsmid, one of the members of the gold fixing, and he had been on the telephone to friends at Standard Chartered throughout the weekend of the JMB crisis, calculating whether any advantage could be gained for Mocatta from the crisis. Jarecki is a tall, shambling figure, whose conversation is quick, entertaining and excitable, and who is distinguishable from other businessmen by a wonderful skill at arbitrage. When he was a medical student in Switzerland he bought gold coins there and sold them across the border in Germany. It was hardly speculation, for he knew he could not lose. Jarecki always hated losing. After a period teaching psychiatry at Yale, he settled for dealing in precious metals and took up Mocatta Metals, where he won more often than he lost, and developed intricate computer programs to minimize risk in the futures market.

The more he thought about the saving of JMB, the crosser Henry Jarecki got. It was, in his view, a decision that stank – not just because Mocatta was now expected to contribute to the indemnity fund but because it represented a missed opportunity. The bullion trade was listless, the gold price was hardly moving, and there were too many new players in the market. The five major bullion banks – the members of the fixing – were all chasing less business. If one of those five was in difficulties, Jarecki saw no sense in saving it. Four members of the fixing would be better news than five as far as he was concerned. When Dr Owen met him a couple of weeks after JMB had been saved, the tale Jarecki told also seemed to have a whiff of scandal to it, which would provide Owen with an opportunity to embarrass the Chancellor. Owen began his campaign with a three-page letter to Lawson. 'It is not clear if the Bank of England was aware,' he wrote,

> that at least some City institutions did not believe that the gold-bullion market, of which JMB is a member, was ever in danger. Nevertheless, a number of questions remain about the propriety of the Bank of England's behaviour and it is in the public interest that a full account of the Bank's role in the rescue of JMB be made by you as the person ultimately responsible for the Bank's conduct as soon as possible. I imagine you were consulted about the £10 million put up by the Bank as part of the overall deal.
>
> The first question is why the Bank, after negotiating successfully a stand-by credit of loans and guarantees to protect depositors and to preserve money-market confidence in the short term, did not then proceed to wind down JMB and ensure a smooth transition to the liquidation of a failed company. Why was it necessary for the Bank itself to take over JMB and all its

159

subsidiaries? Such treatment has not been accorded to a number of other and much larger industrial and commercial companies which have also collapsed in recent years . . .

The most critical question, however, concerns the prospect of public money being called on in future. Although not directly comparable, the total cost to the Bank, and indirectly to public funds (because its dividends to the Treasury were damaged), of the secondary banking crisis ten years ago, was about £100 million. The danger is that the Bank's decision to try and 'turn around' the various businesses of JMB, operating in a difficult, risky and at present depressed market of commodities and precious metals, will inflict in the longer term a similar and potentially even larger toll on both the Exchequer and the taxpayer. The risk of public money being called on in this way is wholly unacceptable because it reflects a Bank of England policy decision which ignores the commercial and market realities confronting JMB.

The Treasury did not exactly leap to the Bank's support. Though Nigel Lawson had been informed of the JMB rescue before the news became public, he had not been consulted during the talks: the decision was not his to take, and any cost would be borne by the books of the Bank. The Treasury's experience led them to believe that in circumstances such as these the Bank tended to expect the direst possible outcome, and would never let a bank go; it was not until some months later that the Chancellor was convinced that the Bank had probably done the right thing. Replying to a parliamentary question on 28 October, Lawson conceded there might be a fault in the system: 'The Bank is considering the lesson . . . if it appears that changes in the statutory framework for banking supervision may be needed I will give this very careful consideration.' In reply to Dr Owen on 31 October, Lawson insisted that the problem did not concern bullion but commercial banking, and no other solution had been possible in the time available. (He added: 'The Bank's judgement is that the prospect for the future viability of JMB's bullion activities is a good deal better than you suggest.') It was a polite and reasonable reply. With a bit of luck that might have ended the correspondence.

But Dr Owen was not satisfied. He replied on 2 November insisting that the Chancellor was wrong about JMB. Contrary to his assertion, JMB's bullion business was bad. Six detailed points followed, and the Chancellor did not answer any of them. He replied on 6 November that Owen's letter had been passed on to the Governor. The unspoken suggestion was that, from now on, the Treasury would prefer the Bank to bear the burden of answering criticism about the rescue. Before receiving the Governor's reply to his letter of 2 November, Owen wrote to Lawson again on 8 November. The transfer of responsibility from the Treasury to the Governor was, he said, 'wholly unacceptable':

> The fact is that you are responsible because taxpayers' money is being exposed, through the Bank's continuing involvement with J M B, with no public accountability or explanation . . . it is imperative in these circumstances that you call the Bank to account for its actions instead of deliberately distancing yourself from the matter.

The Bank had hoped to deflect Dr Owen's offensive by inviting him to talk personally with the Governor: 'off the record, of course'. Owen replied piously that he did not countenance off-the-record conversations, and pressed on. (Capable politicians are exhilarated by running arguments, especially those that get their names in the newspapers.) Letters from him to the Bank of 13 November and 3 December continued to assert that it was J M B's bullion business that had caused its downfall. A somewhat tart reply to the first of these letters, from McMahon on 21 November, hinted at the Bank's edginess. By insisting, contrary to everything the Bank had said, that the bullion business was at the bottom of the collapse, Owen was not only questioning the Bank's competence, but impugning its honour, he wrote. But Owen was relentless. His letter to the Governor on 3 December ended by declaring that he was considering asking the Chancellor to set up a public inquiry.

Pressure for an investigation was building up so fast that the government, seeing that an inquiry was inevitable, set about establishing one which would consider the awkward questions raised by the case discreetly, in private, among people who understood each other. A committee was formed to consider the system of banking supervision, and its chairman was Robin Leigh-Pemberton. The Bank was further represented by Kit McMahon and Peter Cooke. The Treasury representatives were Sir Peter Middleton, the permanent secretary, and Frank Cassell. The one outsider was Deryk Vander Weyer, the former chairman of Barclays who was now deputy chairman of

British Telecom (and who was, incidentally, appointed a director of the Bank a year after the committee reported). The work of the committee might properly be described as essential, or exhaustive, or sympathetic. Independent it was not.

Owen took one last shot at the Chancellor, quoting statistics from a source he referred to as 'my economic advisers'. These were intended to show that bullion was the root of the JMB failure. That he had been advised by Dr Jarecki, a man who had an interest, and that he was eventually proved wrong, did not matter. Dr Owen had set out to embarrass the Chancellor in the Commons and to force him to announce some kind of an inquiry and in this he had been entirely successful.

Back in Threadneedle Street the Bank behaved with a naïve disregard for politics. On 22 November the Bank had transferred £100 million from its own reserves in the banking department to JMB. In banking terms there was a perfectly sound reason for this: JMB needed money to buy foreign exchange to cover potential losses, especially in US dollars, and to give the bank sufficient capital to transact business in the money markets. But no senior figure at the Bank thought it worth mentioning in writing the £100 million transfer to the Chancellor or the permanent secretary. They learned the news from the *New Statesman*, which had received an anonymous tip about the £100 million. The *New Statesman* first checked with the Bank shortly after the Chancellor's announcement of the Leigh-Pemberton inquiry – the action that was designed to put an end to the JMB controversy. Appearing flustered, the Bank at first denied the story. When it did concede that the money had been transferred, the press spokesman insisted that the £100 million was only a short-term deposit: 'We were doing no more in our terms than giving evidence that we were standing behind JMB completely.'

That was what the Bank told the Treasury, and the Treasury was appalled. It knew that the Chancellor's critics would seize on the £100 million transfer as further evidence of JMB's inexhaustible thirst for public money. The Bank could insist that the money would eventually be repaid, but that hardly counted. Lawson felt strongly that he should have been told about the £100 million and let the Governor know it in his customary brutal manner. But his anger was easy to understand. He was in political trouble and the Bank had made it worse. As David Howell, an ex-Cabinet Minister himself, explains: 'When a minister is being held to account, he wants to have control over what he is being held to account for.'

The potential cost to the public purse was rising for a second reason. Negotiations with the clearing banks over the indemnity fund to back JMB's bad debts had dragged on throughout the winter. When the discussions began, the Bank had confidently expected to provide no more than 10 per cent of the fund – the 'small contribution' from public funds that the Chancellor referred to in the Commons on 23 October 1984. Owen had calculated this would amount to £10 million, which he declared was too much. But when negotiations with the clearers, the bullion banks and the acceptance houses were completed in March 1985, and a fund to indemnify losses of up to £150 million had been agreed, the Bank's contribution turned out to be more than 10 per cent. It was, in fact, to be liable for a maximum of £75 million, or 50 per cent of the total. The clearers had agreed to pledge only a little more than the bullion banks (£35 million as against £30 million) and £10 million had been squeezed out of the acceptance houses.

The embarrassing size of the Bank's exposure was the price paid for its deteriorating relationship with the clearing banks. Before he became Governor, there had been murmurs that, as the first chairman of a clearing bank to become Governor, Robin Leigh-Pemberton would be likely to give the clearers an unfair advantage at the Bank. Nothing of the kind happened. Indeed, Conservative Chancellors behaved as though clearing-bank profits were a bottomless pit from which to augment the revenue. The Bank had failed to help the clearers repel these raids by the Treasury, so they owed the Governor no favours. And they had little sympathy for the Bank's predicament. After all, they argued, the Banking Act had been virtually dictated by the Bank, and if that had not been sufficient to restrain JMB, the Bank had no one to blame but itself.

During negotiation about the indemnity fund, middle managers from the clearing banks behaved even less sympathetically towards the Bank than their chairmen and managing directors had done under duress during the JMB weekend. The determination of the clearers to concede the smallest sum possible grew at roughly the same rate as the attacks on the Bank in the Commons. The Bank's authority and its negotiating strength weakened simultaneously. By March 1985 the Bank was down, and the clearers put the boot in. As a last straw, the agreement was not made politely between City gentlemen, but drawn up by highly paid lawyers.

In Whitehall and Westminister, the Bank's standing continued to deteriorate. Caught in a political dog-fight, the Bank did not know how to defend itself. It did not deny its error in transferring £100 million to JMB without telling the Chancellor ('We should have been more alert to the political sensitivities,' says Galpin), but the Governor's admission of this error – which the Chancellor made public in a Commons debate – added to its humiliation. The Treasury, while accepting that Robin Leigh-Pemberton was the last person to wish to deceive the Chancellor, had lost patience with the Bank's naïvety. One Treasury official, who watched the Bank's increasing confusion as the political impact of JMB grew progressively more damaging, observed: 'The Bank is political, but only with a small p.' He compared the time-scales operated by the two bodies: the Bank thinks in terms of continuity from year to year; the Treasury in terms of staying in control of the House of Commons from month to month. Worst of all, the Bank's public image of uncertainty and incompetence opened up the possibility that banking supervision might pass out of the Bank's hands – a possibility almost unthinkable to traditional central bankers like McMahon and Cooke. It was some comfort, therefore, that both were members of the Leigh-Pemberton Committee scrutinizing the supervisors' failure.

The group that was most anxious to give evidence to the Leigh-Pemberton Committee was the Bank of England's bank supervisors. To the supervisors, the real problem was the statute, which was badly drafted and inadequate, and they were glad of an inquiry which would enable them to explain their misgivings. The Leigh-Pemberton Committee met fifteen times, and on twelve occasions heard papers from banking supervision. Many of the supervisors' criticisms of the Banking Act were predictable. They wanted it to cover the work of auditors (who had in this case failed to notice the gaping holes in JMB's accounts); they wanted more power to veto excessively large loans to bank clients; and they proposed that shareholders with more than 15 per cent of the bank's voting power should show their ability to back its assets. They wanted a lot more staff, particularly accountants. But most of all they wanted an end to the two-tier system. The Leigh-Pemberton Committee reported: 'We were told by the banking-supervision division that the administration of the two-tier system had caused considerable difficulties and that a great deal of time and effort has had to be expended in order to apply the criteria fairly and consistently.'

The two-tier system, the report said, had not clearly differentiated between a 'proper' bank, and a less proper bank, a failure which had led to confusion in the public mind. Moreover, the system had allowed two different styles of supervision to develop. Since that was what Gordon Richardson had intended when he lobbied relentlessly for the two-tier system, this was not surprising. 'The styles of supervision have developed somewhat differently,' the report continued. 'Supervision of recognized banks takes account of the experience and standing of the institution and relies considerably on mutual trust and the cooperation of management. The smaller licensed institutions accept and generally appreciate a more direct form of supervision with clearer guidance on the standards generally expected of them.'

The introduction to Leigh-Pemberton's report noted that the committee had not been asked to examine the reasons why the particular problems which arose in the case of JMB had occurred, nor to consider the reasons for mounting the rescue operation, but the next sentence in the report contained a judgement that, while it sounded mild, nevertheless contained a sensational implication: 'JMB's position as a recognized bank was a factor in the delay in the supervisors' becoming aware of, and reacting to, its growing problems.'

This is as close as the Leigh-Pemberton inquiry came to assigning blame, but the implications were not lost on the Bank's supervisors. They were among the few who knew of the origins of the two-tier system, and they fully understood the connection between the tiers and the supervision of JMB. As a top-tier bank, it was assumed to have a management that was experienced, cooperative and trustworthy. Since it was a 'proper' bank, the supervisors were not expected to look for reckless lending policies and dubious clientele. The man responsible for the inclusion of the two-tier system in the Banking Act was, as we have seen, Gordon Richardson. By identifying that system as a factor in the supervisory failure, the Leigh-Pemberton Committee had drawn Richardson into the small group of candidates to whom personal responsibility for the JMB failure could be attributed. The supervisors were privately relieved: 'The two-tier system is our fig leaf,' one admitted later.

If they felt that the Act absolved them from much of the blame, their superiors did not. The supervisors felt great sympathy for their colleague who had been responsible for J M B ('There, but for the grace of God, go I,' was a common reaction), but more senior officials were less sympathetic, and blamed the supervisor herself, sometimes most disagreeably. ('The real problem was that we left it to a damned woman.') The Bank's trade union, B E S O, sensed victimization, and defended her vigorously. (She stayed at the Bank, but was transferred to another department shortly after the J M B weekend.) The fault, the union believed, lay in the institution rather than the individual. Roy Shuttleworth, B E S O's secretary, says: 'If you run an organization on a shoestring with insufficient control, it's inevitable that from time to time there's going to be an almighty cock-up.'

Not all the senior officials at the Bank were so philosophical. Some blamed the relations between Brian Quinn and the supervisors, but the fact that these had taken so long to develop was due to Quinn's role as the Bank's travelling man during the Mexican and Brazilian debt crises. Moreover, Quinn was the number two in the supervisory division: other colleagues wondered what kind of management structure Peter Cooke, the departmental head, had put in place. If he had not been alerted to the failure of a bank to make its quarterly returns, and to the fact that it was prevaricating when prodded, there was evidently something badly amiss in the departmental flow of information. The Treasury was tempted to blame Kit McMahon; and the announcement of his reappointment as deputy governor became the occasion of a petty punishment, being deliberately delayed during the summer of 1985. In the House of Commons a small group of Labour M Ps, of whom the most remorseless was Brian Sedgemore, regularly called for the resignation of the Governor. B E S O sprang to Leigh-Pemberton's defence too. A letter was sent to Sedgemore: 'The pernicious blurring of the edges between events prior to the Johnson Matthey rescue and the Bank's subsequent actions is grotesque. The Governor is widely regarded in the Labour movement throughout the banking industry as an industrious man of the highest integrity and a formidable opponent of tricksters,' the letter said. The Labour front bench was much more circumspect and never mounted a concerted campaign against the Bank: B E S O believed that its intervention with Labour front-bench spokesmen might have influenced the Party's Commons tactics.

By the summer of 1985 Murphy's Law had taken over and everything that could go wrong did so. The Treasury was caught red-handed trying to censor one of its own replies to a parliamentary question. (It tried to retract an admission that there had been 'departure from prudent banking practice' at JMB.) Next, the Bank admitted that its defence of the £100 million transfer had been untruthful. Instead of being a short-term deposit, as the Bank had said, the £100 million had become part of JMB's capital.

To recoup some of the money it had spent, the Bank announced that it would sue JMB's accountants, Arthur Young, for negligence in its inspection of the bank's books. In the Commons Lawson announced that a new Banking Act would follow a Treasury White Paper, and was politely discreet about the reasons for it. ('In general the Bank does a difficult job diligently and well. But in the case of JMB the supervision cannot escape criticism for failing to respond quickly to danger signals.') A new Act might help in the long term, but during the summer months there was a sense of pop-eyed disbelief among politicians, journalists and, indeed, many of the bankers who heard the figures tripping off Nigel Lawson's tongue. JMB had lent a total of £450 million, and of that sum, £248 million – or £55 in every £100 – appeared to be bad debt that might never be collected. It seemed inconceivable that incompetence could exist on such a scale. Surely it must have been fraud? Sedgemore put this question repeatedly in the Commons, until Lawson replied tartly: 'Misreporting, even on the appalling scale that occurred in this case, does not constitute a fraud. That is a point of law.'

Within a month, on 17 July, Lawson was making a statement in the Commons about fraud. The Fraud Squad had discovered serious and unexplained gaps in the records of JMB, 'including the possibility of missing documents relating to substantial past transactions on certain accounts that are subject to large losses'. Though Lawson is not a man who seeks or attracts compassion, it was becoming difficult not to feel sorry for him. But the Chancellor now blamed the Bank again: it had known the Fraud Squad had investigated the affairs of a number of JMB's customers before the takeover in September 1984, but since the Bank had not then owned JMB, it had neglected to pass this information to the Treasury, or to make the information public to show how concerned it was at the possibility of sharp practice. What in fact had mattered to the Bank was that separate Fraud Squad

167

investigations, begun after the bail-out, had revealed no case for prosecution. But what mattered to the Treasury was that once again the Chancellor had been embarrassed in the House of Commons. (Towards the end of the July statement, Sir Peter Tapsell, MP, a shrewd observer of the City, addressed the Chancellor: 'Whatever we do, we should be careful not to reduce the role of the Bank of England to that of the Treasury's poodle.' No such idea had crossed his mind, replied Lawson. The Treasury's cur, perhaps?)

The Bank's latest misdemeanour did not provide a tranquil environment in which to discuss the contents of the Treasury's forthcoming White Paper on banking supervision. The Bank might normally have expected the Treasury to be happy with the conclusions of the Leigh-Pemberton Report – its permanent secretary, Sir Peter Middleton, had been a member of the committee that produced it. But these were not normal times, and the Bank learned, with some dismay, of a new item on the agenda. Martin Hall, the Treasury's man in charge of financial institutions – whose clients included the Bank – had been looking at alternative systems of banking supervision, foreign systems.

The United States's system had not impressed Hall, with its surfeit of supervisory bodies – Federal Reserve, Comptroller of the Currency, FDIC, not to mention state regulatory agencies – though the tradition of vigorous on-site inspection of banks at least once every three years did not seem to him a bad idea. In Paris, Hall had found the French system rather beguiling. A new French banking law in 1984 had created a Banking Commission, which – while the Governor of the Banque de France was chairman – was independent of the central bank. A second body, the Committee on Bank Regulation, established capital ratios, accounting standards and various other technical rules. The policy of the commission and the regulations of the committee were implemented by the supervisory staff of the Banque de France: the central bank executed policy, but did not make it. The French law also authorized on-site inspection by supervisors every four or five years, and gave the Banking Commission the right to refuse the appointment of auditors.

Hall proposed that this be seriously considered as a model for a new British system, and, in doing so, struck at the roots of the Bank's pride and its traditions. The Banque de France was not an institution greatly admired in Threadneedle Street, Bank men finding its subservience to the state unappealing. McMahon was especially indignant at the suggestion, but Hall was not the only Treasury man who thought a banking commission, or board with members from the banking profession outside the Bank of England, a good notion. The Chancellor was also impressed; he was even thinking of divorcing supervision from the Bank and establishing a banking inspectorate. Treasury officials objected to the general absence of commercial experience in the Bank's supervision division, which a few secondments from clearing banks had not altered. The idea of establishing a permanent core of professionalism and expertise in a specialist department was attractive to them, and so was the notion that the body could be made directly accountable to Parliament.

Shortly after the débâcle, Sidney Procter, an experienced commercial banker, had been asked to join the Bank from the Royal Bank of Scotland, but that was not enough to satisfy the Treasury's desire for commercial experience. The Bank was, therefore, anxious to discover what the Treasury had in mind. Was it to be a board like the French one, or an advisory committee? Would the proposed board be telling the Bank what to do, or asking how things were done?

This was the moment at which Lawson could, if he chose, have revenged himself on the Bank. But, having accepted a more pragmatic argument that change would lead to a loss of continuity and to administrative upheaval, he opted not to. The Board of Banking Supervision proposed in the White Paper was intended, Lawson explained, 'to give more forceful direction to the task of bank supervision'. But its powers were 'to assist' the Governor, not to dictate to him. There was, however, a sting in the tail: 'If on any occasion the Governor disagreed with the views of the board's outside members, the Governor would still have the power to disregard their advice. But if he were to do so, he would have to inform the Chancellor of the Exchequer.'

The Governor set up the board right away on a non-statutory basis, and its five members were announced on 15 May 1986. Since their average age was fifty-seven, there was no lack of commercial experience among the three bankers, the accountant and the ubiquitous Deryk Vander Weyer.

Lawson also insisted that the new duties of bankers should be made clear in the new Act. It would leave no doubt that it was wrong to mislead supervisors and unwise to allow a single customer to borrow a substantial percentage of a bank's capital. Until a late stage in the drafting of the new law there were, however, no criminal penalties for transgressors of these guidelines. Then the Prime Minister took a hand. Margaret Thatcher had thoroughly understood the political implications of the JMB affair. Grocers' daughters are not natural sympathizers with rich City financiers, and she is no exception. She told the Chancellor that she thought it ought to be a criminal offence to mislead a supervisor and that banks should be required by statute to advise the Bank of a customer who borrowed more than 10 per cent of its capital base. Statutory provision was also to be made to allow increased cooperation between supervisors and auditors. Speaking in the Commons, Lawson said: 'The system will be strict without being a straitjacket.' Without the advice of his leader, which the Chancellor duly incorporated into the Bill, the statute would not have seemed particularly strict.

The Commons debate on the White Paper just before the Christmas recess was a foul-tempered affair, and reached a climax of a sort in an exchange between Brian Sedgemore and Nigel Lawson. Sedgemore said: 'Is it not time the Chancellor had the bottle to tell the Prime Minister that Pemberton is not merely a disaster, he is a disgrace?'

Lawson shouted back: 'The biggest fraud so far exposed is the honourable member for Hackney South and Shoreditch. He poses as the man who got things moving. He did not even start his seemingly unending series of allegations until 17 July 1985. By engaging in a scurrilous McCarthyite smear campaign under the cloak of parliamentary privilege, to further sordid political objectives, the honourable gentleman is succeeding in damaging the good name of the City, to the delight of our competitors overseas, and impeding the police in their attempt to bring wrongdoers to court, as the police have already pointed out to him. To describe the honourable gentleman as a pest would be unfair to pests.'

Sedgemore's reply – 'You snivelling little git!' – was ignored by the Speaker, but recorded for posterity by Hansard.

This finally lanced the boil. After the debate the pressure on the Bank began to lift, and although the recovery was incomplete and the Fraud Squad's investigations continued, Parliament and newspapers appeared to accept that JMB was a City scandal that would not be ended neatly with the prosecution of a number of guilty men or a satisfactory explanation of how a bank had, it appeared, in a few months in 1984 managed to lose a quarter of a billion pounds.

In fact, the final figures were not that bad. The bullion banking business was sold to an enterprising Australian bullion company named Mase-Westpac for a sum of £17.5 million over net asset value. The Bank was somewhat relieved when the original estimate of £250 million of bad loans, made in September 1984, was reduced to £41.5 million by December 1986. The new management of J M B had been almost as good at collecting debts as the old management had been at contracting them. Abdul Shamji – who had been forced into bankruptcy by the Bank in 1985 – actually paid off his remaining debts: and, at the end, the most significant debt was the many millions lent to Mahmoud Sipra. The Bank's share of the final indemnity fund was £20.75 million, a great deal less than had been feared.

Publication in December 1986 of the annual report of Minories Finance – the name taken after most of J M B's business had been sold to Mase-Westpac – made possible an accurate costing of the price to the Bank of the J M B affair. There was £20.75 million for its half share of the indemnity fund, plus the interest forgone on the £75 million the Bank had injected as new capital into J M B (the original £100 million had included £25 million loan stock, which had been repaid), which over eighteen months would have been about £10 million. So, in cash terms, the cost of J M B was £30 million. There was a chance that the lawsuit against the accountants, Arthur Young, would produce more revenue; none the less a very heavy price had been paid for a failure of bank supervision.

That price did not include the cost of the time devoted to J M B by many senior men in the Bank, nor the cost in terms of the Bank's reputation, authority and morale. It had been a shattering episode for Bank employees; junior staff, making purchases using their Bank of England cheque-books, had been berated by shopkeepers who thought it disgraceful that the Bank should spend hundreds of millions of pounds bailing out a worthless bank. Abroad, the Bank's magisterial image was tarnished. A senior man at the Bank had suggested that I should talk to overseas central bankers to obtain a more mature view than I would get at the time in London. I happened to be in Sydney shortly afterwards and spoke to one of the most experienced officials at the Reserve Bank of Australia. 'Johnson Matthey!' he said sombrely.

171

'It was a great shock. The Bank had a special reputation for *always* knowing what was going on.'

Not all the senior men in Threadneedle Street grasped this, but David Walker, who had been intimately involved in the original rescue, and who became chairman of JMB when Rodney Galpin took over as head of supervision, understood. He observes: 'The fact that the Bank was perceived to be responsible for JMB had a very large negative impact on its ability to do its job, on its prestige, its capacity to exert influence, and, perhaps more than anything else, on its adrenalin – its spiritual energy.'

It also had a profound impact on the careers of many of the people involved. Kit McMahon, having been made to wonder whether he would be reappointed, announced that he intended to become chief executive, and eventually chairman, of the Midland Bank. The JMB affair had turned out to be fully as harrowing as he had feared on the night of the rescue. Though McMahon had a fierce loyalty to the Bank and resented any criticism of it, in the end he was not sorry to go.

Many of his colleagues were surprised that Peter Cooke did not leave as well. The Bank, signalling where it believed responsibility for the failure lay, made him the scapegoat. In the reorganization announced in September 1985 that brought George Blunden back as deputy governor, Cooke was moved downwards and sideways to be an associate director in charge of coordinating international bank supervision, especially in Basle. His place at the head of the supervisory division was taken by Galpin. Brian Quinn remained assistant director in the banking-supervision division.

But when ultimate blame is being meted out, it seems unfair to load it on to the person responsible for operating a system. The system itself was a failure, as the Leigh-Pemberton Committee had found, and responsibility for the débâcle must also lie with the man who had insisted on the basic design: Gordon Richardson. But he was above the fray. Lord Richardson of Duntisbourne was never called on to give evidence in the case.

11

A Conversation with the Governor

The Johnson Matthey affair was a harrowing experience for Robin Leigh-Pemberton. Inside the Bank and the Treasury, no one blamed him, but he was the Governor so he bore the burden of public responsibility. Calls for his resignation from MPs like Brian Sedgemore were easily resisted: he was Her Majesty's appointment, after all. But his authority had been critically undermined. No other Governor of the Bank of England had been asked, in an on-the-record interview, by the man from the *Daily Mirror*: 'Are you up to the job?' (The Governor replied: 'Obviously I suffered a lot of criticism. But it has not affected my determination to see it through.') City gossip was unsympathetic, and money brokers, who ought to hold the Bank in some regard, summed up the Governor's skills by reporting the following conversation:

BANK OFFICIAL: Base rates have changed.
GOVERNOR: Which way?

Rubbing salt in the wound, they compared Leigh-Pemberton with Gordon Richardson – 'a hard man but a banker through and through'. Whitehall gossiped about a meeting of the National Economic Development Council, chaired by Nigel Lawson, at which, though the Governor had a point to make, he was not called. Finally he held up his hand to attract Lawson's attention, but the Chancellor stared through him and called someone else. On the face of it, the story is more revealing about the Chancellor's disagreeable manner, but the fact that it was put about did no good to the reputation of the Governor.

Leigh-Pemberton's reaction indicated that he is a man of character. He recovered quickly from these slights and never whined. After knowing him for a while, Kit McMahon became impressed by a quality that he described as 'inner peace', and he believed that it infused the Governor with real confidence. This enabled him to give the public performances required of him, although he did not always enjoy them. I happened to be in the Commons one day in the spring of 1986 when he was about to give evidence to the Treasury and Civil Service Committee. His face was set and a little pale; he had no time for idle chatter. (One of his aides noted that this was as nervous as he ever gets.) When he sat down to speak it sounded like an ordeal, as though he were a student undergoing an oral exam. An examiner might have said that he was not a conceptualizer; that he got his German interest rates wrong; and that he needed a prompt from Eddie George about the last time the Bank had intervened to prevent the sterling exchange rate rising. Although he had come with something to say, he spoke from the script rather than the guts, except when he was asked to comment on personal taxation. 'I sign a monthly cheque for P A Y E for agricultural workers on my farm and I'm amazed at how much it costs,' he said. (His own wage is £99,550.) He kneaded his fingers and tapped his heels, and when it was over the relief with which he turned to George suggested that he was satisfied at having survived.

In the Governor's spacious room at the Bank he is much more at ease, and one day in the summer of 1986 we had a conversation there. The morning sun had risen over the high façade of the Bank and was slanting sharply through the tall windows leading out into Garden Court. He sat in the shadow behind his desk under Zoffany's portrait of Abraham Vickery (one of the Bank's memorable chief cashiers). He wore rimless spectacles; his grey hair was thick and wavy. He looked the spitting image of the late Kenneth More, the English character actor, and he spoke candidly about the job. He knew, he said, that people were commenting that the Bank had a rather weak Governor and that consequently the authority of the institution was less than it used to be, but he was not cast down. 'I think all Governors have a difficulty to begin with. Lord Cromer, who was Governor in the early 1960s, pointed this out to me. He said: "Take courage, look at what the papers said about me."'

One charge had offended him: the suggestion that he was a political cypher of the Prime Minister's, imposed on the Bank as a punishment because Mrs Thatcher had disliked Gordon Richardson. He hardly knew her, he said. They had met two or three times at Downing Street when he was chairman of the NatWest Bank, and a couple of times when he was vice-chairman of the Kent County Council. 'I have to admit that I went to lunch at Chequers once, but that had more to do with the possibility that I might be made Lord Lieutenant of Kent.' He clearly made a good impression that day.

He was conscious, too, that he had got off to an uncertain start with his old colleagues who ran the clearing banks. He confessed that he had mistakenly assumed that the authority of the Bank depended on the Governor's striking a pose. 'Initially, I felt the dignity of the position required me to maintain some sort of distance, but I accepted, quite honestly, that that wasn't working out. The atmosphere of my

175

routine meetings with the chairmen of the clearing banks has become more informal, easier and much more constructive, and I think my authority as Governor has improved as a result of the more straight-forward and realistic tone I bring to these meetings. I think it is more important that they should realize that I'm exercising my authority on the merits of the situation rather than adopting the stance of the headmaster. I try to be less distant.' A comparison with Richardson was inescapable: I remarked that he had behaved more grandly than a mere headmaster would. 'He was very grand on occasions. He could do it very well,' said Leigh-Pemberton, adding that although he is not grand by nature, and does not believe it is necessary to pretend otherwise, he can be very firm, even rather outspoken, if necessary.

While Richardson represented all the authority of the Bank in his own personality, Leigh-Pemberton lets authority seep downwards to his executives. City talk is that he overdoes delegation: 'I simply approve of everyone doing as much as they can at their own level,' he says. 'I don't like to interfere unduly. I'm satisfied as long as I know the system is working and that the flow of information to the deputy governor, myself and the Court is such that we are able adequately to perform our duty.'

Leigh-Pemberton has a functional definition of the authority of the Bank: it depends on the Bank's being believed to have got things right. By this standard, the JMB affair was a calamity. He was 'surprised, even shattered' by the ferocity of the attack on the Bank in the Commons. 'I don't mind telling you I went through anxious times then. I was well aware that the Bank of England was having one of its low moments. I was watching the television news one night and heard the announcer say: "JMB, into which hundreds of millions have been poured . . ." Hundreds of millions. It was so wrong, I felt like throwing a brick through the screen.

'I felt confident that we would achieve what we were setting out to do, and that when we did that we would come out of it well. On the whole we have. I have acknowledged in public that in banking supervision we failed to pick up signals; there was a failure in communication. Having had this failure I believe we have made the department as foolproof as we can. But I never lost faith in the correctness of the original decision to save JMB. British banking has hardly suffered at all. No depositors lost money, and there was no run on any other bank.'

Would it not be desirable for an outside supervisory body to have the responsibility for overseeing banks? 'As you might imagine,' the Governor replied, 'there are moments when I would dearly like to be relieved of it. Since that has happened in other countries it would be ridiculous to say that we hadn't thought of it, but it was negatived for a very simple reason. Banking supervision has to do with banking supervisors, and the only ones we've got are Bank of England people. A separate body would have to be composed of these people, and we can't force them to leave the Bank.'

What, I asked, is the Bank of England *for*? His reply echoes that of many of his predecessors: 'I suppose primarily it is the guardian of the monetary system, of the currency, and of confidence in it.' I suggested that the Bank of England Act of 1946 had transferred guardianship of the system and confidence in the currency to Her Majesty's Treasury. 'If you have a Treasury that is hellbent on an inflationary programme, I think a central bank has to do its best to reduce the implementation of that policy, to limit as far as possible the damage it does, to advise, to dissuade if possible, to do almost anything except obstruct. I don't think one can obstruct a democratically elected government. If the government decides to go ahead, you have the alternative of executing its policy or resigning.'

He speaks like a man with few illusions. 'I don't hold great store by adopting a remote or restrictive attitude towards people,' he says. He is not so much the Governor, more the chairman of the board. Consequently, he delegates to senior officials: but no matter how good they are at the job, they do not possess, cannot possess, the authority of the Governor. This alters the role of the Bank, since the emphasis is transferred from its image to its professionalism. There is no evidence that Leigh-Pemberton planned this change: it came about because of the differences in personality between Richardson and himself. It does not appear to concern him at all. 'If you're not the man for the job, the truth will emerge,' he says.

This is in character. Leigh-Pemberton is a practical man, informed by his experience. Had it persuaded him that the principal motives in financial markets are greed and fear? 'I think they are more motivated now by the intensity of competition, and that is a simple function of internationalism,' he replied 'For greed, I would substitute pressure to perform. For fear I would substitute anxiety about the new situation. This results from a change in emphasis. It is no longer so easy for a merchant banker to be the guide, philosopher and friend. I do hope that old sentiments will survive and that markets will live by the spirit rather than the letter of the law, enabling us to maintain a flexible approach to regulation. That's been the strength of the London market. It's what visitors from overseas find so attractive about business here. It would be a pity if we were to lose sight of that.'

Unlike Gordon Richardson, whose concern was national and international economic policy, Leigh-Pemberton's preoccupation is with what happens on his own doorstep, especially with the aftermath of Big Bang. 'That's the biggest anxiety, the rectitude of the City. London maintaining its reputation. That's where the biggest risks are.'

12

Ego and Alter Ego

A classic example of the exercise of the authority of the Governor took place shortly before Gordon Richardson left Threadneedle Street in 1983. At the time the behaviour of a number of prominent underwriters at Lloyds had become a subject of scandal, and damaging to the City's reputation. Lloyds was a self-regulating organization over which the Governor had no formal power, so its chairman did not have to appear at the Bank when Richardson asked to see him, nor to appoint a chief executive by the name of Ian Hay Davison at a salary of £130,000 a year, as Richardson suggested. But when the committee at Lloyds learned that that was what the Governor proposed, that is what they did. There was an element of bluff in Richardson's performance, but no one at Lloyds dared call it. As a classic case, it may well prove to have been one of the last of its kind, however. The Lloyds scandal rumbled on; restrictive practices in the stockmarket came under scrutiny; the JMB affair produced a series of shocks and the tin market collapsed. All this helped to reinforce the idea that the financial services provided by the City ought to be regulated not internally, but by law.

As we have seen, Gordon Richardson was a vigorous opponent of the idea of using the law to regulate City business. So were his cronies – men like the influential accountant, Sir Henry Benson. They believed in the doctrine of the thin end of the wedge. They did not deny that dreadful breaches of the City's unwritten rules took place, but believed that to concede that the law was necessary to deal with a particular transgression would give law-makers the opportunity to regulate all the City's activities. That conjured up the example of statutory regulation that haunted bankers and brokers – the Securities and Exchange Commission in Washington DC, which was thought to be full of cheeky lawyers who asked embarrassing questions and insisted on getting the answers.

Richardson referred fondly to the example of the City takeover panel, a non-statutory organization set up by the Bank to see that both sides played fair after one company had bid for another. It had proved a successful exercise in self-regulation, especially under Lord Shawcross. (He had said that the chairman of the takeover panel ought to be a bit of a cad – presumably because it takes one to spot another.) Richardson had hoped it would be a model for further independent, self-regulatory organizations, and pressed for the establishment of a similar body in the stockmarket, the Council for the Securities Industry. But this council never acquired the character that Shawcross had imposed on the takeover panel, and was never taken seriously outside the City.

Moreover, a generation gap was opening at the Bank. Richardson had hired a number of young men, among them David Walker from the Treasury, who was an executive director whose division was entitled Finance and Industry. Almost everything in Britain could be included within that designation, and there was hardly anything about which Walker did not have an opinion. Walker was Richardson's man, but he recalls one area of disagreement between them: unlike Richardson, Walker believed that City regulation by law was inevitable.

His Treasury background made Walker aware of the politics of the argument. He understood that the vogue for consumer protection had now spread as far as the City. The case for investor protection in the securities market was being studied by Jim Gower, formerly a distinguished professor of commercial law at the University of London, who undertook the job at the request of the Department of Trade and Industry. From the outset he was chiefly concerned about methods of regulating securities markets; he did not question the need for regulation.

The stockmarket itself was under pressure from Sir Gordon Borrie, head of the Office of Fair Trading, who had declared unfair the rules of the Stock Exchange, since they included fixed commissions on transactions, and the traditional 'dual capacity' system in which brokers bought shares through jobbers, thus adding to the cost of doing business. In New York brokers dealt directly with each other, using computer technology to buy and sell. When Borrie sought a court order to force the Stock Exchange to end these restrictive trade practices, the brokers and jobbers on the old-boy net proposed fighting the case. To more objective observers like Walker, this decision was a public-relations disaster, symbolizing all that was wrong with the London market. While other markets were becoming more open and competitive, the Stock Exchange was sticking to its old closed ways and losing business to New York. A good deal of blunt talking from Walker was necessary before the Stock Exchange gave up the fight. In return for this, the exchange was given time to adjust. The brokers and jobbers agreed to end 'dual capacity' in October 1986 – a date that became known as Big Bang.

Within a few months of Robin Leigh-Pemberton's succeeding

Richardson, Walker detected an atmospheric change. Gower, Borrie and the approach of Big Bang had all been influential. The Bank had discovered that the 1979 Banking Act, far from reducing its influence, had actually bolstered it. And Leigh-Pemberton was much less doctrinaire than Richardson about the mystical quality of the Governor's authority. By 1984 the nature of the argument had shifted, and was now about the contents of regulatory law rather than about its desirability, for the City had also realized that some legislation was inevitable, and its grandees were concentrating on limiting its importance. The old City establishment in the merchant banks approached Walker and suggested that the Bank should be responsible for implementing any new Act, since it understood the markets.

For generations, the Bank's instinctive response would have been to agree. In 1984 and in 1985, however, it refused. Partly this was realism: had the Governor insisted that the Bank be given wider statutory powers in the City in the wake of J M B, he would have been snubbed. Partly, it was Walker's belief that the preoccupation of the Bank ought to be money, not regulation.

The outcome was the Financial Services Bill and a regulatory organization called the Securities and Investments Board, the S I B. The powers of the Board were circumscribed, however. It could dictate, if necessary, the disciplinary rules to be applied to various City markets, and it could, as a last resort, punish a failure to enforce those rules. But day-to-day regulation was to remain a responsibility of the various markets themselves, in the form of self-regulatory organizations, known as S R Os. Walker describes the system as 'hybrid': for the first time a government-sponsored regulatory organization had a place in the City, but the traditional system of self-government had not been done away with entirely.

The S I B was formally established late in 1985, before the Financial Services Bill finally passed through Parliament in October 1986. Indeed, the S I B played a covert role in amending some of the original clauses in the Bill: Jim Gower, a member of the S I B, provided draft amendments for the Labour Party to propose while the Bill was in committee. In each case, the amendments were intended to increase the power of the board: to insist, for example, on its dictating model rules to the S R Os, and acquiring the power to reject rules that did not conform to S I B standards.

The self-regulatory organizations – the largest being that of the

Stock Exchange – fought hardest to be granted immunity from legal actions brought by members of the market who had been disciplined, arguing that if members of their disciplinary panels were liable for costly actions for damages, no one would be willing to sit on them. Blanket legal immunity is a disagreeable concept in law, but the government was anxious to retain the framework of self-regulation, and eventually conceded it. (The record of the takeover panel was considered good enough for it to be able to lobby successfully to remain outside the orbit of the SIB.) In the end the Financial Services Act was an old-fashioned legislative compromise.

The Bank expressed satisfaction at the outcome and claimed, somewhat rhetorically, to have been the great architect of the new system of City regulation. Its continuing influence would be guaranteed, so George Blunden said, by the right to appoint, in tandem with the Treasury and the DTI, members of the board of the SIB. And the Bank retained its particular monopoly as the supervisor of the wholesale money markets. The effect of these changes on the internal politics of the Bank was to reduce the power of David Walker, who had handed over many of his responsibilities for various markets – like the troubled London Metal Exchange – to the SIB, and to increase the workload of Eddie George's money-market division.

The brokers that had acted for the Bank in the money markets – Seccombe, Marshall and Campion in the discount market and Mullens in the gilt-edged market – were swallowed up, one by Citibank, the other by Mercury Securities, before the Big Bang, and instead of seeking substitutes the Bank declared that it would begin to act as its own broker in the new, competitive markets that resulted from Big Bang. It was a bold decision, but Eddie George is a robust man. Unlike Walker, he had been a Bank man all his life, having been recruited from Cambridge by a man who appreciated his skill as a bridge player (he and the recruiter had played competitively while he was still an undergraduate). George intended to work for the World Bank and regarded his time at the Bank as an apprenticeship, but he married, got a cheap Bank mortgage and rose discreetly through the hierarchy. Having been spotted by Richardson, he was promoted to assistant director in the 1980 reorganization and became an executive director in 1982, at the age of forty-three.

At that time the market for gilt-edged securities was controlled exclusively by British firms and it was in a weakened condition. George decided to end the British monopoly and open the market to all comers. He subjected each of the applicants to a long, searching interview at the Bank and in the process became a familiar figure to them all. The applicants, whether they came from London, Frankfurt, Zurich or New York, found him a model central banker: agreeable, sober, authoritative and reasonably certain he knew best. Eventually twenty-nine were chosen to become market makers and the structure of the market was changed fundamentally.

Since the time when he had established his working relationship with Sir Peter Middleton at the Treasury and Alan Walters at Downing Street, Eddie George had enjoyed a good run. His department was skilfully managing large new issues of government stock, and even won a couple of rounds against the speculators in the foreign-exchange market. He had not been drawn into the maelstrom of the JMB affair, and after Big Bang his responsibilities proliferated: for instance, his division took control of the foreign-exchange operations from the overseas department. So when the Department of Trade and Industry had to decide whether the wholesale money markets – the discount houses and the gilt-edged market makers – were to be supervised by the SIB or by George's department at the Bank, there was no great debate about it. If the Bank's technical competence had been doubted by the Treasury, as was the case from 1979 to 1981, the job could have been appropriated by the SIB, but by 1986 the Treasury was admiring of the Bank's performance in the markets, and the Bank itself had exhibited considerable confidence in its own skills.

George's department got the supervisory job, and this confirmed its élite status: it was now deeply engaged in every activity of the market, from dealing in it to supervising it. Indeed, there was a sneaking suspicion inside the Bank that George might be accumulating too much power. In 1985 the Chancellor had begun to ask the Governor to bring George along to meetings at which the money markets and interest rates were discussed, but late in 1986 the Chancellor's office actually began to bypass the customary channels, simply asking George to pop in to see Lawson. Until George Blunden heard about it, that is. A stickler for the traditions of the Bank and the authority of the Governor, Blunden said that of course Eddie George could drop in to see the Chancellor, but that the Governor and the deputy governor would be dropping in with him.

When they did meet, there were no further doctrinal arguments.

The Governor would fight when he judged that the Treasury was being beastly to the Bank. After the 1986 budget, for instance, the Treasury tried to shift on to the Bank all the blame for an increased tax on ADR's – the mechanism by which British companies sell their shares in the New York market. When a joint statement that offered to share the blame with Whitehall was crossly rejected by the Chancellor, Leigh-Pemberton corrected the Treasury by means of a public statement. His concern was that the integrity and professionalism of the Bank had been impugned by the Chancellor. But the area of disagreement between them hardly ever spread to the economy. The Governor had no desire to make economic policy, only to execute it. But changes did occur. For example, the Treasury downgraded targets for the monetary aggregates like M3 (inflation was under better control despite M3, which persistently rose faster than the official targets), and interest rates were deliberately kept at high levels to offset market pressure for a lower value in the pound (the free market was not to be entirely trusted).

In the struggle for power between Treasury and Bank a truce was called. It was not in Leigh-Pemberton's character to look for a fight. A charming man, he was an excellent public performer, and was away from the Bank for about half the year at Basle (for the BIS), Brussels (for the EEC) and Washington (for the IMF). Besides that, his ceremonial duties as Lord Lieutenant of Kent took up another three to four weeks. Behind the bronze doors on Threadneedle Street more power than Kit McMahon had been able to deploy was being exerted by George Blunden, who had been brought back to the Bank in September 1985 to impose discipline and restore morale after the JMB affair. Both the Governor and his deputy are practical men, made impatient by agonizing and intellectualizing, and before long they became a double act. Blunden had thought the deputy governor's job complemented the Governor's, but experience taught him that they were, in fact, quite similar. While one governor was playing away, the other played at home. The expression 'the Governors' – in the plural – was always part of the language of the Bank, but now it took on a real meaning, and Blunden began to think and behave as if he were Leigh-Pemberton's *alter ego*.

When we talked in the summer of 1986, Robin Leigh-Pemberton declared his chief concerns as Governor – the 'rectitude' of the City and the maintenance of London's reputation as an efficient and clean place to do business. By the end of the year London's reputation for efficiency had just about survived Big Bang (there were inevitable computer foul-ups in the first weeks), but as regards cleanliness, its standing had rarely, if ever, been lower.

In that regard one name was frequently mentioned – the merchant bankers Morgan Grenfell, which had established a reputation in the City for ruthless efficiency, especially in the great takeover boom in the mid-1980s. Soon after Big Bang Morgan Grenfell's chief equities dealer, Geoffrey Collier, was accused of insider dealing and was dismissed. One transgression in an aggressive merchant bank might have been accounted a misfortune, but then Morgan Grenfell became deeply embroiled in the Guinness scandal, which suggested something worse than carelessness.

It transpired that one of the bank's most assertive directors, Roger Seelig, had known about the plot by the Guinness management under the chairmanship of Ernest Saunders to manipulate the Guinness share price so as to assist its takeover bid for the Distillers company. Seelig was sacked. Morgan Grenfell let the City know that, for them, that was the end of the affair.

But at the Bank Blunden was less than satisfied. Of Morgan Grenfell's chief executive, Christopher Reeves, and the head of its corporate-finance department, Graham Walsh, Blunden observed that there were two grounds for their resignation: if they had known what was going on, they were accomplices and ought to go: if they had not known, they were incompetent and ought not to stay. But, despite a growing political clamour over the Guinness affair early in January 1987, Reeves and Walsh gave no sign of leaving. Blunden decided it was time to take a hand.

The rules he applied were a mixture of the new and the old. First he consulted a body of experienced commercial bankers that had been recently established as a consequence of the Johnson Matthey affair – the Board of Banking Supervision. This had begun to sit even before it was formally set up under the new Banking Bill, and he found they supported a move against Morgan Grenfell's top management. Next, Blunden sought out the relevant section of banking law that legitimized Bank intervention in the affairs of Morgan Grenfell – section 17, which states that all banks must be prudently managed. He believed Reeves and Walsh no longer managed prudently. The *coup de grâce*, however, was delivered in the old-fashioned manner, by one of Morgan Grenfell's own outside advisers, a former Governor of the Bank, Lord O'Brien of Lothbury. After meeting Blunden at the Bank he went to see Reeves and Walsh to reveal to them the weapon the Bank could deploy if they did not leave voluntarily. Within twenty-four hours they had gone. The threat of section 17 of the Banking Act was made even more explicit in the removal of Lord Spens from Ansbacher, the merchant bank which had also played a part in the Guinness scandal. The Chancellor of the Exchequer was so encouraged by these events he decided to take some of the credit for them.

While his *alter ego* was looking after the show in London, Leigh-Pemberton was taking the message to the country. Speaking to the Scottish Institute of Bankers on 26 January 1987 he referred to the new Banking Bill, the Financial Services Act and the Securities and Investments Board that it had spawned in terms that emphasized their regulatory power. 'The SIB will be able to set rules of conduct for all investment markets and discipline or expel firms that fail to comply. It will do all of this not on the basis of club rules, but by virtue of statutory powers transferred to it by the government under the Act.' The Governor commented on the fact that the takeover panel was still outside the orbit of the SIB: 'If practitioners do not respect the system, we shall have little choice but to replace it with one incorporating statutory powers of enforcement and statutory sanctions.' Having delivered the threat, Robin Leigh-Pemberton, Governor of the Bank of England, said: 'Our task as regulators is to make the regulation of the City as watertight as it can be.'

No other Governor in the years since 1694 had referred to his role in such a prosaic manner – as just a 'regulator'. Gordon Richardson, in his prime, had chosen squash as an approving analogy because it depended on self-regulation, differences being sorted out without the need for the referee's whistle or the umpire's white coat. Just ten years later his successor was applauding the introduction of statutory legislation and actually threatening to blow the whistle on the City himself.

This provided the Bank with a solution to its problem, for one way of dealing with an identity crisis is a change of identity.

13

Learning New Tricks

By the beginning of 1987 the Bank of England was feeling less sorry for itself. While much of the mystery had evaporated and some of the old authority had drained away, the Bank was gaining new powers. These were vested in it by the Banking Bill which passed through Parliament in the winter of 1986 and 1987. It was the epilogue of the Johnson Matthey affair, and the formal recognition that the Banking Act of 1979 was a poor instrument with which to arm bank regulators. Ian Stewart, the Treasury minister who steered the Bill through the Commons, was perfectly plain about the reason for the failure of the 1979 Act: 'With the benefit of hindsight, as well as foresight, it can be seen that the two-tier structure was fundamentally misconceived.'

Stewart outlined the changes that were to be introduced in the new law: the establishment of a Board of Banking Supervision; the requirement that auditors inform the Bank of potential disasters; that banks identify those customers who have borrowed especially large sums of money; and that bankers wishing to control a bank had to be declared 'fit and proper' by the Bank. The Bank expressed its unswerving support for these measures and the deep rift between the Bank and the Treasury appeared to have closed so neatly that the suspicions of a Conservative backbencher named Anthony Nelson were aroused. He noted that the ex-officio members of the Board of Banking Supervision – the body intended to regulate the regulators – were to be appointed by the Governor, and suspected that this might lead to the formation of a cosy club. 'I question whether we are involved in a cosmetic exercise of setting up a supervisory board to persuade people that something is happening, but, in the end, it will be business as usual.'

Nelson proposed amendments that were more symbolic than real: there should be one more independent member, and the independent members ought to have the right to place before the Chancellor of the Exchequer a record of any disagreement they had had with the Board's executive members – the Governor, deputy governor and executive director for banking supervision. Nelson's intention was to ensure that the Bank would take the Board seriously. Further amendments were intended to improve the Bank's information-gathering system. The original draft of the legislation required shareholders proposing to buy 15 per cent or more of a bank's shares to obtain the permission of the Bank of England. The Bank would then declare the purchaser 'a fit and proper person', or not, as the case might be. To this, M Ps tacked on a further condition: any purchaser of 5 per cent or more shares in a bank ought to be required to reveal his shareholding. Amendments like this were evidence of a lingering suspicion, among MPs who took part in the debate, about the depth of the Bank's commitment to regulation. (These doubts were expressed courteously; vehement critics like Brian Sedgemore and David Owen did not contribute to the closing stages of the debate they had started in 1984 and fuelled during 1985 and 1986.)

These amendments did not impede the steady progress of the Bill through the Commons, but when it reached the Lords, the Bill took on new colouring, becoming the pretext for a daring attempt by the clearing banks and the merchant banks to turn the legislation into a sanctuary in which they could take refuge from bids by bigger and bolder foreign banks. This motive was expressed most clearly by Lord Chandos who asked for an amendment 'to ensure that, when it is deserved, the independence of the major British banks can be protected from unwarranted or unhelpful changes in control brought about by the unchecked workings of the markets . . . There is unease, both in the financial community and outside, that the resources, the power and authority of the Bank of England will need to be enhanced.'

Lord Boardman, who had succeeded Robin Leigh-Pemberton as chairman of the NatWest, asserted that a takeover of a big British bank by a foreign bank would prove to be the thin end of the wedge: 'It would inevitably whet the appetite of other foreign banks . . . I believe that very soon one would find a major part of the British banking system in foreign hands. That would be unfortunate.' That prospect had Boardman's imagination lurching towards even greater horrors: the idea of the Governor having to invite into his inner sanctum the chairmen of Hong Kong, Japanese or German institutions. Lord O'Brien of Lothbury, without invoking such distasteful consequences, nevertheless supported Boardman's case. (Lord O'Brien's successor, Lord Richardson of Duntisbourne, had nothing at all to say in the chamber to his peers about the Banking Bill.)

Early in the debate, government spokesmen argued that the British banks were protected from some predators – the Japanese sprang readily to most minds – by the reciprocity clause of the Financial Services Act that had recently become law. Section 183 of the Act allows the British to blackball financiers from abroad if their own countries do not concede reciprocal facilities for British financiers. This provided little comfort for Lord Elton: 'If Barclays or the Midland, or indeed both, were swallowed by some gigantic Japanese bank, it scarcely protects the national interest – does it? – to know that Lloyds or the Royal Bank of Scotland could acquire in return a fractional percentage of the Japanese system.'

This was the debate over 'the national-interest clause' and it spilled over from Parliament into the Parlours of the Bank of England. To the banking supervisors, statutory protection for the clearers sounded prudent, and, although the bond between the Bank and the clearers was not as strong as before, the traditional relationship still persisted. Consequently, Rodney Galpin, the divisional director, would have welcomed powers to protect the clearers. Eddie George and David Walker were less interested in relationships inherited from the old Bank and argued that the new Bank ought to support a national-interest clause only if it could be demonstrated that it was necessary for the proper supervision of the banks. They did not think it was. As for George Blunden, while he sympathized with the amendment, he saw no reason why an unwelcome predator should not be declared unfit and improper. But he held his hand. To the intense irritation of many bankers in the City, especially merchant bankers, the Bank said nothing to help them secure the national-interest clause.

Without the aid of the Bank, the City bankers were unable to combat the implacable opposition of the Treasury, whose spokesman wondered aloud why it was that clearing banks should be treated any differently from British industrial companies. The only concession from Conservative ministers was a promise that a takeover bid for a British clearing bank would be referred to the Monopolies and Mergers Commission. As concessions go, it was not large. (The clearers were only indulged by the government to the extent of an amendment legalizing the electronic transfer of funds – a system known as EFTPOS).

Back in the Commons, the amended Bill was debated for the last time on 7 May 1987. The Board of Banking Supervision was to have six independent members who would report directly to the Chancellor; all shareholdings in a bank of more than 5 per cent had now to be reported to the Bank; the reciprocity provisions of the Financial Services Act were emphasized for 'the avoidance of doubt'. (Labour members had also persuaded Ian Stewart to raise the amount protected by the Depositors Protection Fund from 75 per cent of the first £10,000 in a customer's account to 75 per cent of £20,000.) Dr Oonagh McDonald, Labour's chief spokesman, who had been obliging throughout the debate, had the last word: 'The main point now will be how the Bank of England uses the powers conferred on it by this legislation.'

The relish with which the Bank deployed its new powers under the Act even before it formally became law on 1 October 1987 indicated a revival of the spiritual energy that had been wasted by the Johnson Matthey affair. There might still be people in Threadneedle Street who believed that banking supervision was not a proper role for the central bank, but it was into the banking-supervision division that bright young men and women and additional cash resources were being channelled. By the end of 1987 there were 180 supervisors, and plans for raising the number to 200 in 1988. Individual supervisors concentrated on fewer banks; computerized reporting systems had been introduced; a small research department was established in the summer of 1987 (one of whose first tasks was to consider the implications of a stock-market crash); and regular staff meetings were held to break down the barriers to communication that had contributed to the Johnson Matthey failure. Accountants received three advisory documents detailing their role in the supervisory system, and their initial suspicion was dissipated when they learned that they were not expected to act as bank supervisors themselves. Once the auditors had begun to provide the back-up system that alerted the Bank to potential troubles, the supervisory division felt reasonably confident at last that it was working with reliable information. This had taken the best part of a decade.

The Board for Banking Supervision had in fact already been operating for eighteen months before the Act became law. Rodney Galpin prepared the agenda for its monthly meetings, and the Bank continued to emphasize its advisory role, but the Parliamentary debates had been a warning against taking the Board too lightly and the Bank was anxious to show that this was not the case. 'If they're strongly of an opinion, it would be most surprising if we weren't persuaded,' says George Blunden. The Board had proved helpful on issues like Third-World debt. By the summer of 1987 the Bank had produced a formula for calculating the sums clearing banks ought prudently to write off as bad debt. (Indeed, banks became so enthusiastic about writing off debt that, by the beginning of 1988, the Governor had to warn them against an excess of eagerness, fearing it might persuade the debtors to forget about their liabilities altogether.)

Blunden himself was determined to turn the Banking Act to the advantage of the Bank, viewing the statute as an opportunity rather than a punishment. Blunden saw that the Bank now had the right, established in law, to dictate who should and who should not control a bank, which was more power than it had had when the Governor raised his eyebrows. Within months of the passage of the Act, Blunden was receiving prospective bank purchasers at the Bank and laying down the new law. Maurice Saatchi had astonished the City by announcing that the advertising business had much to teach commercial banking, and that the Saatchi brothers would like to make a bid for the Midland Bank. Saatchi, calling on Blunden to explain his case personally, was told that the proposal was unwelcome: the Bank considered him and his brother neither 'fit nor proper'. Robert Maxwell was told much the same thing when he proposed himself as the white knight who could save the small merchant bank, Guinness Mahon, from the clutches of a New Zealander, Ron Brierley.

To make sure the new code was widely understood the Governor put the Bank's policy on the record in a speech on 13 October 1987: 'I would need some persuading before an industrial or commercial company is allowed to take control of a bank.' Furthermore: 'We do not look favourably on acquisitions of stakes designed to put banks "into play" solely with the view to making a quick investment gain. Neither do we welcome bids whose purpose is to gain control so that a bank may be sold or broken up.' Robin Leigh-Pemberton named no names, but the ears of Lord Hanson (with a stake in the Midland) and the Australian, Larry Adler (a holding in Hill Samuel) may well have been burning.

The Governor's boldest statement, however, appeared to contradict the Treasury view that there was no need to build defences that would protect a British clearing bank from foreign predators: 'We should, I believe, be ready to accept that the public interest requires continuation of a strong British presence in our key domestic money, credit and capital markets.' Uncoded, this meant that the Governor was no more enthusiastic than Lord Boardman at the prospect of sharing his table with the heads of Hong Kong, Japanese or German institutions.

The Governor's statement had the impact of an *ex cathedra* statement, but in fact the Banking Act had undermined the authority of the Bank as well as bolstering it. In the past, there had been no appeal

194

against a powerful Governor's ruling. Now the Bank's powers depended on legal interpretation: if any applicant did not agree that he or she was 'unfit' or 'improper', the Bank would have to justify its decision before a tribunal and, if necessary, the court of appeal. This was uncharted territory. (For instance, it was uncertain whether an appeal would be heard in open court.) So the Governor's public assertions and the deputy governor's private admonitions were based, in part, on bluff. If the victims of their judgement began to test it in the courts, the Bank would naturally become more circumspect about applying it.

For the time being, however, the Act boosted the Bank's confidence, and when it was tested by the collapse of the bull market on Black Monday, 19 October 1987, the Bank behaved with assurance. Interest rates were lowered to ensure that no participants were squeezed by the cost of borrowing money, and the search for casualties was carried out discreetly under Brian Quinn, the assistant director of the banking-supervision division. Within days it became clear that two market makers were in distress: Barclays de Zoete Wedd (BZW) and County NatWest. Both dealt in securities in the London and New York markets; at the time neither was regulated, though both would eventually come under the supervision of the Securities and Investments Board in 1988 when it finally became operational.

But both BZW and County NatWest were subsidiaries of clearing banks. When their problems were identified, the Bank's supervisors became anxious about the possible impact of the losses in the securities subsidiaries on the soundness of the parent banks. To satisfy themselves about Barclays and the NatWest, the Bank's supervisors had to reassure themselves about the management and balance sheets of two of the leading players in the London securities industry. By accident, the crash of '87 forced the Bank to trespass on the SIB's territory. The Bank, whose relations with the SIB had been strained by the formal, legalistic style of its staff, saw an opportunity to extend its influence, and did not hesitate to take it.

One troubling repercussion of the crash was the confusion that arose over the sale of the government's shares in British Petroleum. The banks that underwrote the issue had set the share sale price before the crash, and when that price fell along with all the others the banks were threatened with losses that might prove ruinous for some, especially the American and Canadian investment banks and securities houses. At the eleventh hour Nigel Lawson intervened with a scheme

195

to limit the underwriters' losses: the Bank of England would guarantee a floor price. Before making the announcement, the Chancellor was apprehensive, fearing that he might be accused of bailing out wealthy bankers and brokers. But the scheme was well received, and the Chancellor applauded. Only one thing diminished Lawson's satisfaction and that was a report suggesting that the brilliant scheme was not his idea at all, but the Bank of England's.

In fact, during the ten days before the Chancellor's announcement the Treasury and the Bank had each appreciated the need for a scheme of some kind, but they could not discuss details because the Bank had a formal, semi-legal position as arbiter in any dispute between the Treasury and the underwriters. Only on the day of the Chancellor's announcement were the two parties able to talk to each other, and they then discovered that they had independently reached the same conclusion: that the issue department of the Bank should offer to buy back the shares. They disagreed about the price at which these shares should be bought, and the Chancellor took the Treasury's advice on that score rather than the Bank's.

Anyone might find it galling to see his clever idea being attributed to someone else, but the level of Lawson's outrage recalled the paranoia that had characterized the relationship between the Treasury and the Bank earlier in the decade. Lawson curtly and publicly informed the Governor that while he had no quarrel with him, he ought to control his people. Both sides slid back into their trenches. The Bank denied that it had ever claimed credit for the BP buy-back scheme ('It's untrue and a malicious lie') while privately blaming Bernard Ingham, the Prime Minister's press secretary, for aggravating the affair in order to remind the Bank of its subservient position.

However little the Bank might have been to blame for that fracas, it was still capable of executing self-inflicted wounds. Shortly after the BP business, an American painter named J. S. B. Boggs appeared in court to answer charges that he had illegally reproduced a British banknote. Boggs is a painter of banknotes; he does it well, and there is a market for his canvases. This prosecution was brought privately by the Bank under Section 18 of the Forgery and Counterfeiting Act of 1981, after the Metropolitan Police had declined to bring the case, there being no suggestion that Boggs had forged or counterfeited the notes. (He always signed his own notes.) Boggs's crime was to have failed to procure the permission of the Bank of England before he painted them. He had actually asked twice, and twice been refused, but the Forgery and Counterfeiting Act, unlike the Banking Act, contained no provision for an appeal against the Bank's ruling and the refusal had been made with an effortless display of arrogance by a middle-ranking official in the banking department.

The prosecution was brought by the banking department to sustain its authority; no one in the department seemed to question whether the case might not rather undermine that authority by exposing it to ridicule. None of the senior officials of the Bank was given an opportunity to express an opinion one way or another. The Bank's argument was put by Graham Kentfield from the banking department (Boggs's lawyer described Kentfield as a man 'whose brow doubt had never furrowed'), and it swayed the judge, in whose opinion the case was open and shut. The jury, however, was not persuaded that the Bank's authority was incontestable. Its verdict was that Boggs was not guilty. The Boggs prosecution showed that the old Bank men had not entirely faded away. Indeed, a few of the Bank's traditional attitudes seem unalterable by time.

When I first visited the Bank in 1978, I asked to see the gold vaults. I was taken two floors below Threadneedle Street, to an iron gate where my identity was established before I was admitted to an office with rings of large keys hanging from the wall. That was as far as I was going. 'A reputation for being as safe as the Bank of England is not easily come by,' I was told – the chief cashier did not want writers describing the vaults, however discreetly, in case it gave anyone ideas. All I learned on that occasion is that the vaults are on two floors and cover a total of three acres. A year or so later I was taken to see the vaults at the New York Federal Reserve Bank (where, incidentally, I believe I saw more money in one place than anybody since Midas – gold was at its peak price of $825 an ounce, and the bullion in that room was valued at around $225 billion). In New York the guards were armed, but relaxed, and said that if I could pick up one of the ingots and run with it, it would be mine.

There had been many changes in attitude at the Bank between 1978 and 1986, so I was hopeful when I asked a second time whether I could see the vaults. I was told to present myself for this purpose one Wednesday in June; again I went down, past the office I had sat in before and through a steel door into a large dank room. It was for

197

short-term storage and along one wall was the day's trade in gold bars
in small stacks, looking more like chocolate bars than bullion. Along
another wall stood display cases showing bars from various refineries
round the world, all at least .9995 pure gold. They came in different
shapes, the Australian ingots, for instance, being square rather than
bar shaped. There was also a display of gold coins, including the rare
£2 piece of 1817. These were museum pieces, however, and I was hoping
to see the real thing – the storehouse of gold which one insider had
hinted might be even larger than the New York Federal Reserve or
Fort Knox. (The Bank is a repository for the gold of other nations and
central banks as well as for the British gold reserves.)

'Could we go into the vaults now?' I asked. 'Sorry,' said my
guide, 'the banking department gave me permission to take you no
further.' There was no point in arguing. I remonstrated later with
senior officials; though they seemed sympathetic, no new date was
fixed. Eventually I learned that the chief cashier had put his foot
down again: no visiting writers. There is still nothing as safe as the
Bank of England.

The impenetrability of the vaults is one of the prime examples of
the old Bank mystique, along with the pink coats and red waistcoats.
Gordon Richardson was the embodiment of that Bank. Recall his
remark: 'I do think (the office of Governor) commands a certain degree
of goodwill. It's true of Prime Ministers and Popes too, isn't it?' It is
impossible to imagine Robin Leigh-Pemberton feeling the least bit like
either a Prime Minister or a Pope. The institution can no longer support
such grandeur.

The Bank no longer emphasizes the pink livery or its gorgeous
furnishings in its recruitment literature. The stress is on professionalism
– a clear departure from the style of the gentlemen of the Bank of
England. Young men and women entering the Bank are informed that
its authority rests on their skills and not their bearing. In Threadneedle
Street today this is defined as 'the need to win the argument'. The
assumption that the Bank can no longer get away with statements *de
haut en bas* is part of the City revolution. Though it does remain as a
ghostly presence, like the outline of a medieval painting on a church
wall, the Bank's mystique has all but vanished. Its authority, once a
creation of the Bank's style and confidence, is now buttressed by the
law, and in the execution of monetary policy the Bank more often
than not acts as the skilled agent of the Treasury. But the Bank was

one of the last English institutions to retain a dignity commensurate with a position and destiny in the Empire, as Sir Herbert Baker had put it sixty years ago. It is not a matter of regret that it has gone. The wonder, rather, is that the Bank was able to cling to it for so long.

While the transition was taking place it was painful, but it happened quickly. By the end of Robin Leigh-Pemberton's first term only fifteen years had elapsed since the rudimentary system of banking supervision had been run by the principal of the discount office and a staff of fifteen. In the meantime, the Bank's influence over economic policy had waxed in the 1970s, when it witnessed the demise of Keynesianism and the conversion to pragmatic monetarism, and waned in the 1980s. But while these cyclical shifts took place, banking supervision became much too important to be left to the discount office.

When the banking-supervision division was established, it was considered by the élite policy-makers to be a humdrum business, but the most significant part of the story of the last fifteen years in Threadneedle Street concerns the movement of the bank supervisors from a position on the fringe to the centre of the new Bank's activities. We have seen how the beginnings of the shift were accompanied by a lack of enthusiasm, and how that absence of conviction led to the passage of an inadequate Banking Act in 1979; how the Johnson Matthey affair scarred the Bank by the dramatic revelation of its inadequacies, and finally how they were reviewed and corrected. There is not a great deal of romance about banking supervision, but learning to take it seriously and getting it right has been the burden of the Bank's past decade, and that was reflected in the choice of the man to run it.

Robin Leigh-Pemberton's term was due to end in June 1988. The government normally announces its intentions about the governorship six months before the end of a term, which means that speculation begins almost a year earlier. True to form, in July 1987, the *Observer* confidently announced that Leigh-Pemberton would not be reappointed. Some weeks later the *Daily Telegraph* asserted with equal confidence that he would be. Some senior merchant bankers expressed with startling passion their hope that he would be going. (He stood accused of having insufficiently protected their interests.) Inside the Bank most of his colleagues hoped he would be staying. This was not just because he is an agreeable figure. It was because the collective leadership formed by the governors, Eddie George, David Walker and Rodney Galpin, was working well. If Leigh-Pemberton were to leave, the candidates for the succession would include George and Walker. If either became Governor (or left because he did not), the whole team would be shattered, when it was common sense to keep it intact.

Following the *Observer* story, Leigh-Pemberton placed a call to Whitehall; not to the Chancellor but to Sir Robert Armstrong, the Cabinet Secretary, and the man with immediate access to the Prime Minister, who appoints the Governor. Leigh-Pemberton wanted to know whether there was any truth in the story of his departure. Within an hour Armstrong reported that there was not, and that the Prime Minister would be delighted to have him stay. The decision was up to him.

Leigh-Pemberton's reappointment for a further five-year term was announced on 28 January 1988. The *Financial Times*, which had described the original appointment as 'a cause for concern', was now a little kinder, welcoming the second term with faint praise: 'There is no doubt that the last five years have marked a transition by the Bank. Whereas it used to exercise its authority through informal means, it now derives its powers largely from statute. But a modernization of the Bank's role was also desirable – at least in some areas – and Mr Leigh-Pemberton's contribution to the process may well be that he has gracefully facilitated what was inevitable anyway.'

There was no way of forecasting it, but the collective leadership that had been a rationalization of the Governor's reappointment had broken up before the winter was over. David Walker was appointed chairman of the Securities and Investments Board, and Rodney Galpin was to leave to become chairman of the troubled Standard Chartered Bank. Walker's appointment was a bold one, rather like asking a clever board director at Marks and Spencer to run Tesco: the business is the same, but the style is entirely different. The S I B's first chairman, Sir Kenneth Berrill, had irritated the Bank by his independent and legalistic approach. In Threadneedle Street, Berrill stood accused of having sacrificed efficient markets in favour of investor protection. The Bank favoured a more nimble-footed technique which protected investors without appearing to enfeeble the markets, and under the new management of Lord Young, the Department of Trade and Industry, which had previously supported Berrill, became more sympathetic towards the Bank's view. Young himself favoured the appointment of an industrialist, but when his candidate – Alan Clements, ICI's finance director – turned him down, he no longer opposed the joint view of the Chancellor and the Governor that the right man was David Walker. The Governor had mixed feelings about letting him go. Walker's original kind of forceful manner made him the countervailing power to Eddie George in the collective leadership, which would inevitably be weakened by his departure, at least for a time. But when Walker's appointment was announced on 26 February, the common reaction was to assume the Bank was extending its power: that from now on the SIB would be managed in a way that would not cause the Bank discomfort, especially when it was also announced that Walker would retain his directorship, with a seat on the Court.

His colleagues asserted that had Rodney Galpin been offered the chairmanship of the Standard Chartered Bank two years earlier, the Governor would not have let him go. Standard Chartered was a worry, but its management problems were not particularly difficult to analyse, and Galpin was not the only man in the City of London capable of solving them, but during the period of recovery from the Johnson Matthey affair Leigh-Pemberton had come to admire the tough and uncompromising manner exhibited by Brian Quinn. The succession to Galpin, whose new job was announced on 4 March, was made easier by the removal of Peter Cooke from the list of candidates; he had resigned in February. Quinn succeeded Galpin and Walker was succeeded by Pen Kent from the International division. (Both, incidentally, had been the Bank's spokesman as head of the information department.)

The balance within the collective leadership shifted, but the sanguine front presented by the Bank about the consequences of these changes, together with the reappointment of the Governor, suggested that it had actually been transformed into an organization that depended on its professional techniques. The old Bank's style had reflected the personality of the Governor. Much of its independence derived from the splendour of the Governorship, and that had been surrendered. The Bank was really independent only as long as people inside the Bank believed in its independence. These days, not many do. They are nearly all new Bank men now. In fact, this new corporate style gave the Bank of England the stamina it needed to survive the turmoil of the 1980s.

The Old Lady had learned some new tricks.

A Note on Sources

This is not an academic work and I have not larded the text with footnotes. I should, however, like to acknowledge my sources of information. Of course, I did use written sources and these are mentioned below, but a great part of the material in this book comes from interviews, mostly conducted during the first nine months of 1986.

In 1978, I wrote an article about the Bank of England for the *New Yorker*, and this provided me with a simple method: to talk to as many people in the Bank as would give me their time. I have counted forty-nine men and women in the Bank who spoke to me formally. (I can think of only two senior staff members to whom I did not speak.) The Bank of England Staff Organization arranged meetings with members of the staff I might otherwise have only seen in the corridors. I also spoke to a number of people who have left or retired from the Bank.

I found most of the people anxious to help – quite literally, since I often felt that, like me, they were trying to discover what kind of institution the Bank has become. There were a number of occasions when I walked out on to Threadneedle Street thinking, 'Why are they telling me all this?'; 'they' were not being mischievous or indiscreet, for they appeared as interested in arriving at the answers to some of my questions as I was myself. Nor did the Bank's officials flinch when they were asked to confirm conversations that I incorporated in the manuscript. All this was not the case with officials who are still employed at the Treasury, who insisted on anonymity. Those ministers and civil servants who had left the Treasury were less inhibited.

It would be laborious to name all the people I saw at the Bank, but I would like to thank Sir Kit McMahon, who argued persuasively in favour of my projects first in 1978 and again in 1985, when I approached the Bank a second time. Once the idea had been agreed in principle, I was helped most generously by the heads of the information department at the time, first Brian Quinn and then Philip Warland. Without ever compromising their loyalty to the Bank, they acted like my advocates. It is the fault of neither that I have not seen the gold in the vaults. Carolyn Smith, who is Philip Warland's assistant, displayed great dexterity with my timetable.

What follows is a list of the published sources I used. Publishing details are in the Bibliography.

Prologue: A Crisis of Identity

The history of the Bank of England sports club entitled *The House* is an exhaustive account. It was published by the Bank in 1986 and it is a bargain for students of the relationship between banking and amateur sport in the twentieth century.

Chapter 1: Mystery on Threadneedle Street

A complete bibliography of books about the Bank of England would be remarkably short. This is a commentary on the Bank's discretion since, until recently, it has preferred to help only a select group of distinguished economic historians to write official histories. Sir John Clapham began the task with two volumes dealing with the Bank's early history, published in 1944. R. S. Sayers continued the story, with a further two volumes, and a volume of appendices, published in 1976. Both respected the Bank's official modesty, and present a largely uncritical view of the history. Despite the fact that it was published over a hundred years ago, Walter Bagehot's *Lombard Street* is a good introduction to the style as well as the history of the Bank.

The literature on the Governors is even slimmer. Montagu Norman cultivated a sense of mystery about himself, which was cracked only when Andrew Boyle published his biography in 1967. Norman flits in and out of a delightful memoir of life in the Bank by Herbert de Fraine, entitled *Servant of This House*. Other tales of the Bank are like collectors' items, discovered by chance in books like *Great Morning*, the third volume of Osbert Sitwell's autobiography. One modern source of these fragments is *The Old Lady of Threadneedle Street*, the Bank's quarterly staff magazine. Any story of the British currency is also a history of the Bank and I used the most recent of these, by Joe Cribb. The rich verbal history of the Bank was passed from one generation to the next by old Bank men. Few new Bank men share this enthusiasm. I soon found I knew more anecdotes about curiosities of the Bank's history than most of the younger people I met.

Chapter 2: The Nation's Money

Accounts of the Bank's activities appear regularly in its own learned journal, the *Bank of England Quarterly Bulletin*. These never recognize the role of individuals in the application of policy. Indeed, most do not identify the author. An article published in the *Bulletin* in March 1982 titled 'The role of the Bank of England in the money market' is the best official account of that activity. The annual reports of the Bank are unappealing documents, but they do record personnel changes, and contain much useful statistical information. Since the passage of the Banking Act in 1979, a section of the annual report is devoted to the work of the banking supervision division. To my knowledge, the only person who has made a joke about funding government debt is Jock Bruce-Gardyne (now Lord Bruce-Gardyne of the *Sunday Telegraph*). Consequently, any description of the Bank's operations must be drawn almost wholly from observation. This has been permitted only in the past ten years.

Chapter 3: Leslie O'Brien: Last of the Gentlemen

Written records of economic policy since 1970 are mostly either anecdotal – as in the diaries of Cabinet ministers – or academic. Charles Goodhart collected the papers he published in the *Quarterly Bulletin* and reprinted them with an interesting linking commentary in *Monetary Theory and Practice*. Although Michael Moran is an academic, his book, *The Politics of Banking*, is written in a style designed to satisfy a wider audience. His book is subtitled 'The Strange Case of Competition and Credit Control', but its scope is broader than that: it gives an intelligent and clear account of the Bank's preoccupations throughout the 1970s. Moran can be read for pleasure as well as instruction. Evidence to the Wilson Committee which reviewed the functioning of financial institutions was published in the *Bulletin* in 1978; and Gordon Richardson's evidence to the Commons Select Committee on Nationalized Industries on 18 January 1978 was printed by HMSO.

HMSO also published, in May 1982, the *Report of the Crown Agents Tribunal*, a remarkably irresponsible government publication, which drags the reputation of many upstanding figures down into the mire. This makes it compelling reading. However, important parts of the secondary-banking-crisis story are still available only in conversation with the participants.

Chapter 4: Gordon Richardson: Elegant Meritocrat

My interest in the Bank was aroused by my first visit to Threadneedle Street in 1978. Together with my then colleague, Hugo Young, I was compiling an account of the 1976 sterling crisis. This appeared in the *Sunday Times* on three Sundays in May 1978, and was later published as a pamphlet entitled *The Day the £ Nearly Died*. This was my first acquaintance with many of the characters in this book, and since then I have squirreled away information about that episode. John Fforde's speech about the origins of monetarist policy, titled 'Setting Monetary Objectives', was reprinted in the *Quarterly Bulletin* in June 1983.

Chapter 5: A Law to Separate Sheep from Goats

As the story gets longer, the list of published sources becomes shorter. Michael Moran is good on the origins of the Banking Act. The Committee of London Clearing Banks' evidence to the Wilson Committee contains early evidence of the Bank's diminishing reputation in the City. Hansard's record of the debates on the Banking Bill reveals little about its origins: that was obtained most succinctly from its originators.

Chapter 6: Operating in a Stylish Way

Statistical information about the Bank's organization and hierarchy appears each year in its *Report and Accounts*, published in May. To discover what is really happening in the pecking order at the Bank it was necessary to talk to the participants.

Chapter 7: Humbling the Great Panjandrum

Sir Alan Walters's account of Margaret Thatcher's economic policy is titled *Britain's Economic Renaissance*. I found it both uncritical and inaccessible; Walters was much more rewarding in conversation. The alternative view to Walters's is expressed most trenchantly by William Keegan each Sunday in the *Observer* and in his *Mrs Thatcher's Economic Experiment*. David Howell gives a good account of the same experiment in *Blind Victory*. The Monopolies Commission report on the bids for the Royal Bank of Scotland was published in January 1982 (Cmnd 8472).

Chapter 8: The Romance of Central Banking

The account of Montagu Norman's dramatic intervention in Austria's economy comes from Andrew Boyle's biography of Norman. Roy Assersohn describes the Bank's role in the Iranian hostages affair in *The Biggest Deal*. Andreas Whittam-Smith wrote a sympathetic description of Gordon Richardson's role in the Mexican debt crisis in the *Daily Telegraph* on 1 June 1983, but most of the evidence had to be drawn from the memories of the participants.

Chapter 9: Johnson Matthey Bankers: the Horrors Begin

Hugh McCulloch's advice to bankers has been privately printed by the Bank. The longest account of the affair of Johnson Matthey Bankers appears in the Bank of England's annual report for 1985, and it runs to no more than ten pages. Describing the build-up to the bail-out has been largely the work of journalists so far. Granada TTV's 'World in Action' produced two programmes on the business career of Abdul Shamji in October 1986. An interesting account of the bail-out was broadcast on BBC Radio Four on 1 October 1985. Parliamentary debates were the other useful source. The Bank itself has remained reticent in the years since the bail-out on the pretext that it is engaged in a legal action against JMB's accountants.

Chapter 10: A Drain on Spiritual Energy

Hansard is still the best source for the events that followed the bail-out. Dr David Owen's office was quick to provide copies of his correspondence with the Chancellor of the Exchequer. Two government publications considered the implications for the Bank's supervisory role: first was the report of the committee set up to consider the system of banking supervision – the *Leigh-Pemberton Report* (published in June 1985, Cmnd 9550). Next came the Treasury's White Paper on *Banking Supervision* (in December 1985, Cmnd 9695). Inevitably, my account relies heavily on interviews at the Bank and the Treasury and in the Houses of Parliament.

Chapter 11: A Conversation with the Governor

The Governor appeared before the Commons Treasury and Civil Service Committee on 14 April 1986 (his evidence was printed a week later).

Chapter 12: Ego and Alter Ego

Big Bang resulted in more books about the City appearing in a single month than had appeared in the previous generation. These paid scant attention to the Bank of England, however. The *Quarterly Bulletin* in December 1985 contained a useful article by Patricia Jackson entitled 'Change in the Stock Exchange and Regulation of the City'.

Chapter 13: Learning New Tricks

The debates on the Banking Bill appear in the House of Commons Hansard (28 November 1986; 19 February, 7 May 1987); House of Lords Hansard (3, 16, 23 March; 6, 27 April 1987) and in eleven sittings of the Commons standing committee between 11 December 1986 and 5 February 1987. The best account of the Boggs case is by Lawrence Weschler and appeared in the *New Yorker* on 25 January 1988.

Bibliography

Assersohn, Roy, *The Biggest Deal*, London, Methuen, 1982

Bagehot, Walter, *Collected Works*, vol. 9 (*Lombard Street*), London, The Economist, 1978

Boyle, Andrew, *Montagu Norman*, London, Cassell, 1967

Bruce-Gardyne, Jock, *Ministers and Mandarins, Inside the Whitehall Village*, London, Sidgwick & Jackson, 1986

Bond, A. J. N., and Doughty, M. O. H., *The House, a History of the Bank of England Sports Club, 1908–1983*, Roehampton, Bank of England Sports Club, 1984

Cooper, John, *The Management and Regulation of Banks*, London, Macmillan, 1984

Clunn, Harold P., *The Face of London*, London, Phoenix House, 1951

Cribb, Joe, ed., *Money, from Cowrie Shells to Credit Cards*, London, British Museum Publications, 1986

Ferris, Paul, *Gentlemen of Fortune*, Weidenfeld & Nicolson, London, 1984

de Fraine, Herbert G., *Servant of This House; Life in the Old Bank of England*, London, Constable, 1960

Goodhart, C. A. E., *Monetary Theory and Practice, the UK Experience*, London, Macmillan, 1984

Howell, David, *Blind Victory*, London, Hamish Hamilton, 1986

Keegan, William, *Mrs Thatcher's Economic Experiment*, London, Allen Lane and Penguin Books, 1984

Moran, Michael, *The Politics of Banking*, London, Macmillan, 1984

Sayers, R. S., *The Bank of England, 1891–1944*, 3 volumes, Cambridge, Cambridge University Press, 1976

   Central Banking After Bagehot, London, Oxford University Press, 1957

Sitwell, Osbert, *Great Morning*, London, Macmillan, 1948

Walters, Alan, *Britain's Economic Renaissance; Margaret Thatcher's Reforms, 1979–1984*, New York, Oxford University Press, 1986

Index

FOR THE BEST IN PAPERBACKS, LOOK FOR THE 🐧

In every corner of the world, on every subject under the sun, Penguin represents quality and variety – the very best in publishing today.

For complete information about books available from Penguin – including Pelicans, Puffins, Peregrines and Penguin Classics – and how to order them, write to us at the appropriate address below. Please note that for copyright reasons the selection of books varies from country to country.

In the United Kingdom: For a complete list of books available from Penguin in the U.K., please write to *Dept E.P., Penguin Books Ltd, Harmondsworth, Middlesex, UB7 0DA*

In the United States: For a complete list of books available from Penguin in the U.S., please write to *Dept BA, Penguin, 299 Murray Hill Parkway, East Rutherford, New Jersey 07073*

In Canada: For a complete list of books available from Penguin in Canada, please write to *Penguin Books Canada Ltd, 2801 John Street, Markham, Ontario L3R 1B4*

In Australia: For a complete list of books available from Penguin in Australia, please write to the *Marketing Department, Penguin Books Australia Ltd, P.O. Box 257, Ringwood, Victoria 3134*

In New Zealand: For a complete list of books available from Penguin in New Zealand, please write to the *Marketing Department, Penguin Books (NZ) Ltd, Private Bag, Takapuna, Auckland 9*

In India: For a complete list of books available from Penguin, please write to *Penguin Overseas Ltd, 706 Eros Apartments, 56 Nehru Place, New Delhi, 110019*

In Holland: For a complete list of books available from Penguin in Holland, please write to *Penguin Books Nederland B.V., Postbus 195, NL-1380AD Weesp, Netherlands*

In Germany: For a complete list of books available from Penguin, please write to *Penguin Books Ltd, Friedrichstrasse 10 – 12, D–6000 Frankfurt Main 1, Federal Republic of Germany*

In Spain: For a complete list of books available from Penguin in Spain, please write to *Longman Penguin España, Calle San Nicolas 15, E–28013 Madrid, Spain*

FOR THE BEST IN PAPERBACKS, LOOK FOR THE 🐧

A CHOICE OF PENGUINS AND PELICANS

The Second World War (6 volumes)   Winston S. Churchill

The definitive history of the cataclysm which swept the world for the second time in thirty years.

1917: The Russian Revolutions and the Origins of Present-Day Communism
Leonard Schapiro

A superb narrative history of one of the greatest episodes in modern history by one of our greatest historians.

Imperial Spain 1496–1716   J. H. Elliot

A brilliant modern study of the sudden rise of a barren and isolated country to be the greatest power on earth, and of its equally sudden decline. 'Outstandingly good' – *Daily Telegraph*

Joan of Arc: The Image of Female Heroism   Marina Warner

'A profound book, about human history in general and the place of women in it' – Christopher Hill

Man and the Natural World: Changing Attitudes in England 1500–1800
Keith Thomas

'A delight to read and a pleasure to own' – Auberon Waugh in the *Sunday Telegraph*

The Making of the English Working Class   E. P. Thompson

Probably the most imaginative – and the most famous – post-war work of English social history.

FOR THE BEST IN PAPERBACKS, LOOK FOR THE (penguin logo)

A CHOICE OF PENGUINS AND PELICANS

The French Revolution Christopher Hibbert

'One of the best accounts of the Revolution that I know . . . Mr Hibbert is outstanding' – J. H. Plumb in the *Sunday Telegraph*

The Germans Gordon A. Craig

An intimate study of a complex and fascinating nation by 'one of the ablest and most distinguished American historians of modern Germany' – Hugh Trevor-Roper

Ireland: A Positive Proposal Kevin Boyle and Tom Hadden

A timely and realistic book on Northern Ireland which explains the historical context – and offers a practical and coherent set of proposals which could actually work.

A History of Venice John Julius Norwich

'Lord Norwich has loved and understood Venice as well as any other Englishman has ever done' – Peter Levi in the *Sunday Times*

Montaillou: Cathars and Catholics in a French Village 1294–1324
Emmanuel Le Roy Ladurie

'A classic adventure in eavesdropping across time' – Michael Ratcliffe in *The Times*

Star Wars E. P. Thompson and others

Is Star Wars a serious defence strategy or just a science fiction fantasy? This major book sets out all the arguments and makes an unanswerable case *against* Star Wars.

FOR THE BEST IN PAPERBACKS, LOOK FOR THE 🐧

A CHOICE OF PENGUINS AND PELICANS

Dinosaur and Co   Tom Lloyd

A lively and optimistic survey of a new breed of businessmen who are breaking away from huge companies to form dynamic enterprises in microelectronics, biotechnology and other developing areas.

The Money Machine: How the City Works   Philip Coggan

How are the big deals made? Which are the institutions that *really* matter? What causes the pound to rise or interest rates to fall? This book provides clear and concise answers to these and many other money-related questions.

Parkinson's Law   C. Northcote Parkinson

'Work expands so as to fill the time available for its completion': that law underlies this 'extraordinarily funny and witty book' (Stephen Potter in the *Sunday Times*) which also makes some painfully serious points for those in business or the Civil Service.

Debt and Danger   Harold Lever and Christopher Huhne

The international debt crisis was brought about by Western bankers in search of quick profit and is now one of our most pressing problems. This book looks at the background and shows what we must do to avoid disaster.

Lloyd's Bank Tax Guide 1987/8

Cut through the complexities! Work the system in *your* favour! Don't pay a penny more than you have to! Written for anyone who has to deal with personal tax, this up-to-date and concise new handbook includes all the important changes in this year's budget.

The Spirit of Enterprise   George Gilder

A lucidly written and excitingly argued defence of capitalism and the role of the entrepreneur within it.

FOR THE BEST IN PAPERBACKS, LOOK FOR THE

A CHOICE OF PENGUINS AND PELICANS

Lateral Thinking for Management   Edward de Bono

Creativity and lateral thinking can work together for managers in developing new products or ideas; Edward de Bono shows how.

Understanding Organizations   Charles B. Handy

Of practical as well as theoretical interest, this book shows how general concepts can help solve specific organizational problems.

The Art of Japanese Management   Richard Tanner Pascale and Anthony G. Athos   With an Introduction by Sir Peter Parker

Japanese industrial success owes much to Japanese management techniques, which we in the West neglect at our peril. The lessons are set out in this important book.

My Years with General Motors   Alfred P. Sloan   With an Introduction by John Egan

A business classic by the man who took General Motors to the top – and kept them there for decades.

Introducing Management   Ken Elliott and Peter Lawrence (eds.)

An important and comprehensive collection of texts on modern management which draw some provocative conclusions.

English Culture and the Decline of the Industrial Spirit   Martin J. Wiener

A major analysis of why the 'world's first industrial nation has never been comfortable with industrialism'. 'Very persuasive' – Anthony Sampson in the *Observer*

A CHOICE OF PENGUINS AND PELICANS

A Question of Economics Peter Donaldson

Twenty key issues – the City, trade unions, 'free market forces' and many others – are presented clearly and fully in this major book based on a television series.

The Economist Economics Rupert Pennant-Rea and Clive Crook

Based on a series of 'briefs' published in the *Economist* in 1984, this important new book makes the key issues of contemporary economic thinking accessible to the general reader.

The Tyranny of the Status Quo Milton and Rose Friedman

Despite the rhetoric, big government has actually *grown* under Reagan and Thatcher. The Friedmans consider why this is – and what we can do now to change it.

Business Wargames Barrie G. James

Successful companies use military strategy to win. Barrie James shows how – and draws some vital lessons for today's manager.

Atlas of Management Thinking Edward de Bono

This fascinating book provides a vital repertoire of non-verbal images – to help activate the right side of any manager's brain.

The Winning Streak Walter Goldsmith and David Clutterbuck

A brilliant analysis of what Britain's best-run and successful companies have in common – a must for all managers.

FOR THE BEST IN PAPERBACKS, LOOK FOR THE

PENGUIN BUSINESS

Great management classics of the world (with brand new Introductions by leading contemporary figures); widely studied business textbooks; and exciting new business titles covering all the major areas of interest for today's businessman and businesswoman.

Parkinson's Law or **The Pursuit of Progress**   C. Northcote Parkinson
My Years with General Motors   Alfred P. Sloan Jr
Self-Help   Samuel Smiles
The Spirit of Enterprise   George Gilder
Dinosaur & Co: Studies in Corporate Evolution   Tom Lloyd
Understanding Organizations   Charles B. Handy
The Art of Japanese Management   Richard Tanner Pascale & Anthony G. Athos
Modern Management Methods   Ernest Dale & L. C. Michelon
Lateral Thinking for Management   Edward de Bono
The Winning Streak Workout Book   Walter Goldsmith & David Clutterbuck
The Social Psychology of Industry   J. A. C. Brown
Offensive Marketing   J. H. Davidson
The Anatomy of Decisions   Peter G. Moore & H. Thomas
The Human Side of Enterprise   Douglas McGregor
Corporate Recovery   Stuart Slatter